Lee Gatiss 'preaches the word'  as he expounds 2 Timothy and Titus, applying the scriptu[ ]. Like Paul, he urges those in min[ ] and courage ready to reprove, [ ] times. While he calls on the w[ ]ness of earlier generation[ ] of great teachers, he clearly addresses the present context and his strong and lively words challenge us to live and speak for Christ however unpopular that may be. Read it to be strengthened.

PETER JENSEN
Former Archbishop of Sydney and General Secretary of GAFCON

Paul's words to Timothy: 'fulfil your ministry' are as relevant and urgent today as they were when Paul first wrote them. As I eye the finish line, I am grateful to Lee Gatiss for drawing me back again and again to Paul's words and for helping me think through their application both for myself and for those of the next generation that I am privileged to train.

MERVYN ELOFF
Rector of St James Church Kenilworth, Cape Town, South Africa

This biblical exposition of the Pastoral Epistles arose out of practical experience, and experience in teaching others to teach others. It is a valuable guide and encouragement for both pastors and laity, and is written in a style that all can easily understand. We warmly recommend its use in the church.

BEN KWASHI
Former Bishop of Jos (Nigeria) and GAFCON General Secretary

If you are exploring the idea of paid gospel ministry, or you have been a minister for many years; get this short commentary, dig into 2 Timothy and Titus, and be mightily encouraged. Dr Gatiss offers so many realistic insights to the challenges of ministry from the text that will help you be better prepared for the long haul.

ANDY FENTON
Director of 9:38, Raising Up Global Workers

There is no doubt that these are difficult times for evangelical churches and evangelical ministers. Our culture long ago turned away from its Christian heritage to become hostile to the gospel, and large swathes of the institutional church have abandoned the apostolic faith once-for-all entrusted to the saints. Addressing these challenges head on, Lee Gatiss gives a stirring call from 2 Timothy and Titus to ministers to have confidence in the gospel and to be willing to suffer for it. Given his role as Director of Church Society, many applications inevitably have a specifically Anglican context, but the principles he expounds are just as relevant to those ministering in other ecclesiological traditions. Many non-conformist denominations are facing the same pressures to compromise and need faithful and courageous leadership just as much as the Church of England, and can learn much from those who are standing firm in national and global Anglicanism. He highlights the vital need for ministers who exhibit Christ-like character and practice personal godliness and purity. The many examples from church history of gospel faithfulness in previous generations are inspiring, and far from being depressing the exposition is full of hope because the gospel is true and Jesus has already won the victory over sin and death.

JOHN STEVENS
National Director of the Fellowship of Independent Evangelical Churches (UK)

The Pastoral Epistles have been a source of support, guidance and encouragement to Christians who are discerning how to respond to the call of God on their lives. Lee Gatiss opens the Word of God in these Epistles with a comprehensive depth and in a manner that will bring clarity and confidence to the reader. This book is a treasure for both lay and ordained.

JULIAN M. DOBBS
Bishop of the Anglican Diocese of the Living Word (USA)

Gatiss's faithful exposition and insightful application conveys the power of God's Word to revive pastors and pastors-to-be for such a perilous time as this. It will kindle 'fire in your bones' for the gospel—its defence and its proclamation!

RENNIS PONNIAH
Former Bishop of Singapore

# FULFIL YOUR MINISTRY

## 2 Timothy and Titus and the Challenges of Serving the Gospel

## LEE GATISS

CHRISTIAN
FOCUS

Copyright © Lee Gatiss 2024

paperback ISBN 978-1-5271-1161-5
ebook ISBN 978-1-5271-1180-6

10 9 8 7 6 5 4 3 2 1

Published in 2024
by
Christian Focus Publications Ltd,
Geanies House, Fearn, Ross-shire,
IV20 1TW, Great Britain.

www.christianfocus.com

Cover design by
Daniel Van Straaten

Printed and bound by
Bell & Bain, Glasgow

# Contents

# Introduction

These are difficult days for those who pastor God's people. In many parts of the world, especially in the West, culture and society have turned away from their Christian past, as if from something both passé and repulsive. Churches are profoundly divided over how to cope with this disorientating situation, and there is much unseemly confrontation. It is no wonder then that many people who might previously have considered giving their lives to full-time ministry in the church are now uneasy and uncertain at the prospect. And yet it is at just such a time—when huge swathes of the population are ignorant of even the basics of the faith, and churchgoers are often left confused and bewildered by the deep public rifts in the church—that we need trustworthy spiritual guides.

Being a pastor today can be tough. John Calvin remarked that gospel ministry 'is a laborious and difficult charge; and that they who aim at it should carefully consider with themselves, whether or not they were able to bear so heavy a burden. Ignorance is always rash; and a mature knowledge of things makes a man modest.' This is not something to rush into. Men and women without ability or wisdom often aspire so confidently to hold the reins of secular government, he says, but we ought to restrain such rashness in the church. 'It is no light matter to be a representative of the Son of God in discharging an office of such magnitude,' he warns, 'the object of which is to erect and extend the kingdom of God, to procure the salvation of souls which the Lord himself hath purchased with his own blood, and to govern the Church, which is God's inheritance.'[1] What we need are pastors who appreciate the seriousness of this task, and yet have confidence in God to strengthen them for it.

Paul wrote 2 Timothy and Titus for this very reason. These are letters from an apostle, a missionary church planter, and a pastor of great experience to his trusted younger colleagues. Yet as the Presbyterian commentator David Dickson (1583–1662) says, Paul wrote 2 Timothy so that 'all teachers may learn how they ought to duly discharge the ministry of the gospel.'[2] Like many today, Timothy and Titus were facing huge challenges in serving the gospel, trying to keep their churches safe from charlatans and false teaching while doing the work of an evangelist in places famously full of idolatry, immorality, and entrenched opposition. Paul's letters gave them the guidance they needed in such a moment, to keep them on track.

Erasmus once said (paraphrasing 2 Timothy), 'there are perilous times at hand because of some who, under pretence of godliness, turn true godliness upside down, and so boast of themselves, as though the Christian religion consisted in words and not rather in pureness of heart.'[3] Is it not true that we remain in such perilous and precarious times for the gospel? No wonder many are often wary of entering full-time ministry today.

I am convinced that these God-breathed words contain vital instruction for us today, especially for those who are considering or just starting out in the demanding work of gospel service. I have preached on them many times in different places around the world, and always found them to be richly rewarding and edifying for my own soul as

---

1. John Calvin, *Commentaries on the Epistles to Timothy, Titus, and Philemon* (ed. William Pringle; Bellingham, WA: Logos Bible Software, 2010), pp. 73–4 on 1 Timothy 3:1.

2. Lee Gatiss and Bradley G. Green (eds.), *1-2 Thessalonians, 1-2 Timothy, Titus, Philemon* (Reformation Commentary on Scripture; Grand Rapids: IVP Academic, 2019), p. 215.

3. Gatiss and Green (eds.), *1-2 Thessalonians, 1-2 Timothy, Titus, Philemon*, pp. 212–13.

well as those I was preaching for. Every year for nearly a decade I spoke on them at the Junior Anglican Evangelical Conference (JAEC) for men and women who were either considering ministry, training for it, or in the early stages of full-time service in the church.[4] I have also edited the Reformation Commentary on Scripture volume on the Pastoral Epistles, which involved a delightful deep dive into the historical interpretation of these Pauline letters. The chapters in this book therefore have something of an Anglican and Reformational flavour to them at times, though not, I hope, in a way that would be too distracting for readers from other traditions. It is my prayer that they may enlighten, enliven, and inspire a new generation to 'preach the word… in season and out of season' (2 Tim. 4:2) and pass on the gospel 'to reliable people who will also be qualified to teach others' (2 Tim. 2:2 NIV).

May this book help you to 'fulfil your ministry' (2 Tim. 4:5), discharging all its many difficult duties—for the glory of God and the good of the world.

LEE GATISS
Cambridge

---

4.    You can find out more about JAEC at www.churchsociety.org. A few of the expositions in this book have appeared in an earlier form in books published by Church Society emanating from that conference.

# 1

# Shamelessly Suffering for the Gospel
## 2 Timothy 1:1-10

2 Timothy is probably the Apostle Paul's last letter. It is quite a personal one, to his trusted co-worker Timothy. And the first thing that Paul mentions in this personal letter, after 'the promise of life that is in Christ Jesus,' is Timothy's spiritual heritage, and his own spiritual heritage. They both had believing ancestors who brought them up to love God, and who prayed for them, no doubt every day. The first message Paul has for Timothy as he launches into this letter is 'be faithful to our spiritual heritage.' That's the thrust of verses 1-7 of this opening chapter.

### Be faithful to our spiritual heritage

What Paul actually says, when you boil it down, is that he thanks God for Timothy's faith. So verse 3, 'I thank God... as I remember you' and verse 5, 'I am reminded of your sincere faith....' But there's more to it than just 'Paul thanks God for Timothy's faith.' He must be letting us in on his prayers for a reason. And I think it's to do with the little asides he inserts into his thanksgiving. He's appealing to shared memories, and to his intimate knowledge of Timothy's family and history.

Have you ever noticed the way that Paul reminds Timothy of his spiritual heritage in verse 5? 'I am reminded of your sincere faith, a faith that dwelt first in your grandmother

1

Lois and your mother Eunice....' Timothy is just one in a line of believers in his family. He's not an isolated Christian. There's a history here, people who came before him who laboured over and prayed for and worried about his spiritual health.

Paul knows that too of course. Verse 3: 'I thank God whom I serve, *as did my ancestors,* with a clear conscience...' He too had a believing family. So both Paul and Timothy are part of something bigger than just themselves as individuals. They had faithful families, and are part of an ongoing work of God which spans the generations. They were not just serving a cause that started a few decades ago.

Paul is also reminding Timothy of their time together. They had developed a close relationship through working together on the mission field over many years. So Timothy is, says Paul, 'my beloved child.' Or as he puts it in his first letter to Timothy, 'my true child in the faith.' Paul wasn't literally his dad, biologically. But spiritually speaking he was like a father to him.

And Paul remembered Timothy's tears, when they had parted. They were close. That's implied by the fact that Paul knows the first names of Timothy's mum and grandma too, of course. Just think about that—can you name your friends' mums? What about their grandmothers? I think we're often closest to those whose families we have some acquaintance with. And Paul wants to remind Timothy at the start of this letter that they're intimate friends.

There's a big stress on memory here actually. Paul thanks God when he *remembers* Timothy in his prayers. He *remembers* his tears, verse 4. He's *reminded,* verse 5, of his sincere faith. This talk of memory and reminders is all leading to the persuasive reminder of verse 6. 'For this reason'—because of our spiritual heritage and our shared spiritual history—'I remind you to fan into flame the gift of God.' Where he's come from, all they've done and been through together, gives Paul the way in to encourage this young pastor. But notice the tone of Paul's remarks. It's not a heavy-handed command or a patronising reprimand from the great apostle to the young convert. Paul appeals to him from alongside him. That's his 'rhetorical angle.' Not above, but beside the younger man.

He reminds Timothy in verse 6 of a significant moment in his life and ministry when hands were laid on him. I think that's probably the same event described in 1 Timothy 4:14 where the council of church elders laid hands on him and he received some kind of gift, probably the spiritual gift of leadership of the church at Ephesus. Paul was there on that day when Timothy started on this path. So his appeal to Timothy is from beside him—not just as the great apostle, which he was by the will of God, but as his partner in ministry and fellow-worker. He reminds him that he was given a gift that needs to be continually fanned into flame.

God did not give us, he says, a spirit of fear—the word can also be translated 'cowardice' or 'timidity.' He's saying that when God equipped him for ministry, He didn't give him the Spirit of spinelessness. Or actually, he doesn't say that, does he? He says 'God gave *us* a spirit not of fear but of power and love and self-control.' It's not just about Timothy, but about Paul too: 'God gave *us*....' As if Paul is also reminding himself of God's empowering, strengthening his own resolve not to shrink back or be a coward in the face of suffering and hardship.

He's saying again: be faithful to *our* spiritual heritage and inheritance. We've been given the Spirit of power, love and self-control. Just what's needed at a time like this. Just what we need as ministers of the gospel, says Paul. We'll need *power*, just to keep going as Christians, especially if we have to suffer for it. Paul tells Timothy to suffer for the gospel 'by the power of God.'

And we'll need *love* when people in the church are difficult to deal with. Anyone who has been in ministry for a few years can testify that the sheer, youthful enthusiasm for the job wears off after a while, but if you love the people

3

God has put in your care, then that sustains you and compels you. But we also need *self-control*, as Paul says, so we don't fly off the handle at our theological opponents, but keep our heads in the face of heresy and immorality. Such things are as inevitable as the annual tax return, and can be just as frustrating. Yet we're not to run to the whisky or to social media to cope or procrastinate. God has given us the Spirit of self-control.

So I don't think it would be fair to say that Timothy is timid by nature, as some people seem to assume. He was one of Paul's most trusted, well-trained, and respected colleagues. If he was scared by the slightest thing then he wouldn't have survived very long in Paul's mission agency, would he? No, Paul is saying that God has given *us* everything we need for this difficult task, Timothy. So let's both of us keep going! It may not be easy—and we'll come to why that is in a moment—but let us press on.

They have a shared spiritual heritage. Paul is confident of Timothy's faithfulness. But heritage requires loyalty, and confidence needs to be validated—in both their cases. As a good preacher I'm sure Paul is preaching to himself in verse 7 just as much as he's preaching to his co-worker. Neither man can afford to sit on his laurels as it were.

I wonder if it would be possible to apply this to us? Let's be faithful to *our* spiritual heritage and fan into flame the gift of God that we've been given, however dimly it might be burning at present. Let's keep the flames of humble, prayerful, careful study of God's Word alive in our day, just as it's been handed down to us over many years by our spiritual forebears. Let's not be afraid to work hard at it, and let's not grow weary in the battles, for God did not give us a spirit of fear, but of power, of love, and self-control.

I know this is addressed to an individual, Timothy, and not to a church. But it would be a great message for churches which have a history of solid biblical ministry. Let us be faithful to our spiritual heritage. Let's remember those men and women of the faith who stood for biblical truth and passed it on faithfully to us. Our families perhaps, our mentors, our children's church teachers, our camp leaders perhaps.

It would be great to go on and ponder how this might apply to denominations too. Can we call the Church of England, my own denomination, back to be faithful to its spiritual heritage? Can I appeal to my fellow Anglicans by reminding them of those great theologians and bishops like Thomas Cranmer, Nicholas Ridley, and Hugh Latimer— the evangelical doctrines they placed in our constitution, and died to defend? Will the Church of England be faithful to that heritage, or shrink back, so that instead of power and love and self-control we end up merely with worldly compromise, superficial nicety, and rampant immorality?

Can we apply it to the wider evangelical world too? We have a heritage of standing firm on the Bible, on the cross, and on evangelism. Many seem to be going wobbly on these core commitments today. Evangelicals were once united on such doctrines and on biblical morality. Nowadays there are so many fault lines in our constituency that I sometimes wonder whether the only thing which unites us is opposition to gay marriage. And in some evangelical circles, even that seems to be weakening.

An evangelical bishop said to me recently that he feared we were now clear on homosexuality but utterly divided and at war over the Atonement. And that this was wrong, and totally at odds with our spiritual heritage. I fear he may be right. But it's so easy to be timid, to be tempted to shy away from that kind of internal controversy, when we really need to be united on the things we *can* be united on. As the bishop spoke, I could feel in myself a tendency to want to smooth over such differences for the sake of an apparent unity on a pressing issue of the day. But part of me also whispered that it would be difficult for me to read or preach this passage, if I wasn't prepared to apply it to the struggles I face in my own ministry. The question kept coming back—will I be timid for the sake of an easy life, or be faithful to our spiritual heritage as evangelicals?

Well, I don't know if we can apply it like that. But it would be interesting to try. Yet we must press on and look at the second part of this opening chapter, and particularly at verse 8. It's a key verse for understanding this whole letter actually, so we'd better spend some time unpacking what it says. I think what verse 8 is saying is: Let's suffer together without shame.

## Let's suffer together without shame

Because of our great spiritual heritage and history and inheritance, let's suffer together without shame, Paul says: 'do not be ashamed of the testimony about our Lord, nor of me his prisoner, but share in suffering for the gospel by the power of God...' Suffering is a big theme in 2 Timothy. Paul himself is in prison as he writes the letter, on trial because of his preaching of the gospel. And he warns Timothy later on in 2 Timothy 3:12 that 'all who desire to live a godly life in Christ Jesus will be persecuted.'

So the temptation is to be ashamed. Ashamed of what? Don't be ashamed 'of the testimony about our Lord.' Or as he calls it later in the verse, 'the gospel.' The good news of Jesus Christ our Lord. Don't be ashamed of it. Don't water it down, or ignore bits of the message, or leave out the unpopular bits. Don't be ashamed of it, whatever people say or do.

And then, more surprisingly, he says don't be ashamed of *me*. Don't be ashamed of Paul? Well, it's one thing to call people to be loyal to Jesus and His Word, but surely Paul is going a bit far now? Has he got one of those narcissistic personality disorders, that you sometimes see in celebrity pastors (or those who would like to be celebrities)? Jesus was the Messiah, the Son of God Himself. But Paul? He's just a man.

Well, we're going to come back to that thought in the next chapter, because it deserves careful attention. But let's think for a moment first about how Timothy might have been ashamed of the testimony, the gospel, of Jesus. There are several reasons, after all, why he might have shrunk back from a full-blooded, wholehearted commitment to the gospel.

For a start, it was a message about a crucified Messiah. And a crucified Messiah wasn't a very popular idea in a context where crucifixion was reserved for the lowest of the low. 'The utterly vile death of the cross' (as the early church theologian Origen referred to it) wasn't spoken of at all in polite society without a twinge of disgust. Crucifixion was reserved for barbarians, slaves, and peasants—the scum of the earth.[1] So to worship a crucified God was simply 'madness' in this context—ancient writers called Christianity a 'sick delusion' and 'a senseless and crazy superstition.' Why would anyone want to worship a crucified God?

And there's evidence that some churches did indeed back off the idea. Paul had to remind the Corinthian church, for example, about the cross—not as something to be ashamed of but as something to be proud of. Because in that moment of apparent weakness and helplessness, Christ defeated death and took the punishment that our sins deserve. So perhaps Paul is reminding Timothy here not to go the route of those Corinthians—whom Timothy knew well—and be ashamed of the cross where our Lord was killed like a lower-class criminal. If people were contemptuous of the cross, we'd be tempted to downplay it wouldn't we? Not to forget it altogether in our theology of course, but to emphasize some other, less distasteful element of the testimony about our Lord.

I think that has resonance for us today. You will have heard perhaps of modern preachers who wish to domesticate the message of the cross, so that its offensiveness is blunted. They want to take away all thought of God punishing Jesus

---

1. See for example, Martin Hegel, *Crucifixion* (London: SCM, 1977), p. 34.

in our place, of Jesus voluntarily bearing the righteous anger of God against our sin so that we can go free. They don't like it when they hear the standard Reformation truth in Article 2 of the Church of England's *Thirty-nine Articles* which says Jesus died 'to reconcile his Father to us.' They think that should just be the other way around.

Others want to sacrifice the idea that Jesus saved us from judgment and hell, on the altar of a more culturally acceptable universalism. Others want to turn the cross into the Christian equivalent of a Che Guevara T-shirt—a symbol of heroic sacrifice, or an emblem of social revolution. But Paul calls us to resist such moves to make the cross more palatable, or even trendy.

There are hints in chapter 2 of this letter that Timothy's opponents in Ephesus are moving towards a more spiritualized version of the gospel, which would downplay or deny things like sin and judgment and suffering. But, Paul says, don't be ashamed if our message is unacceptable to the world. Don't be ashamed if it means you have to suffer taunts and insults, if believing in Jesus and especially His substitutionary death appears to be intellectual suicide to your contemporaries or unexciting to your congregation.

The Church of England's Declaration of Assent, which clergy have to make when they are ordained, calls Anglican ministers to be loyal to the inheritance of faith that we have received. Our inheritance of faith—that is, the *Thirty-nine Articles,* the *Book of Common Prayer,* and the Ordinal—is meant to be our 'inspiration and guidance under God' for all our evangelism and ministry. But has such loyalty to confessional formulas (whether Anglican, Baptist, or Presbyterian) gone out of fashion? The idea of straightforwardly keeping your ordination vows, even when it hurts—is that outdated and un-Christian?

I love the idea of loyalty. It is a noble and majestic word. It has connotations of unswerving allegiance, trustworthiness, dependability, fidelity. All good things. In love, in war, and above all in ministry, loyalty to the truth requires the ability to stick one's neck out. And God did not give us a spirit of fear in such situations, but a spirit of power, of love and self-control.

But I wonder if there are other things we are tempted to be ashamed of? A few years ago, I emailed a dozen of my contemporaries from theological college and told them I was preaching on this passage. I asked them if they were tempted to be ashamed of Jesus in any way. I got some very interesting responses! Now, none of these guys are shrinking violets. They are all competent and energetic in the work. But the surprising thing is, they all knew exactly what Paul means in verse 8 here. They're all tempted to be ashamed.

One passionate evangelist said to me: 'When I'm explaining the gospel one-to-one or in small groups, it dawns on me what a silly idea it is.' What goes through his head is, quote: 'They'll never fall for this.' And when he's preaching evangelistic sermons, he says: 'I always feel myself blushing as I mention sin and … when I plead with people to repent and believe, I have this nagging thought— what is the point, stop now, make a benign application and don't make a fool of yourself.'

Another friend, who is usually pretty forthright and straight writes: 'A non-Christian friend says to me "Your church doesn't tell people they're going to hell does it?" … I wonder why I pause so long before I say something. I stumble out something that isn't too bad. But the pause says it all—I'm ashamed of the truth because I don't want to look bad in this guy's eyes.' Another friend confessed, 'I'm ashamed of Jesus' hatred of sin and love for holiness.' He didn't want to have to talk about *that* in the hedonistic, pleasure-seeking context he works in.

An Australian minister friend had this very revealing story to tell: 'I was once out with friends from a Beach Mission team when we were accosted by dangerous looking youths (we're all descended from convicts you know). They surrounded us and started shoving me. I was figuring out who to hit first and how we would look after the girls with us. My five-foot nothing tiny slip of a friend started saying "You don't need to hit us. Don't you know Jesus loves you? I'd love to talk to you about him." They were so embarrassed they ran away. The shameful thing is that I was embarrassed too. I'd rather have been involved in a fist fight than show myself as weak and talk about Jesus.'

Have you ever met a shy, embarrassed Australian? A Sydney Anglican one? And yet contemplating speaking up for Jesus can silence even the most ardent Christian. Especially if there's suffering involved—whether loss of face or loss of blood. My friends had more to say about being ashamed of the Apostle Paul, so we'll come back to them again in the next chapter.

Paul's exhortation to Timothy is spot on, isn't it? God did not give us a spirit of fear. Don't be ashamed. Not because Timothy is a weakling or a timid little mouse, but because he's an ordinary Christian experiencing the powerful pull of temptation in a God-hating, anti-Jesus culture. Just like us.

And Paul calls Timothy to share in suffering for the gospel. Again, that tone of being alongside Timothy is evident here. He coins a new word in verse 8 which means 'share in suffering' or 'suffer together with us.' Jesus suffered, says Paul. I'm suffering too. Join with us in suffering for the gospel; be faithful to *that* spiritual heritage.

Let's be loyal to Jesus, like the long line of men and women who have been reviled, ill-treated, imprisoned, exiled, silenced, burned ... for not backing away and keeping quiet. Read Eusebius's history of the early church, or Foxe's book of Reformation martyrs, or the stories of those who were tortured for Christ in Cold War Eastern Europe, or who died for being Christians in Pol Pot's Cambodia, or who stood up to impure anti-Christian tyranny in Uganda. We're part of a family, a movement, which has never been short of suffering. We follow a Messiah who said 'Take up *your* cross, and follow me.'

This should have great resonance for those of us who treasure the Reformation (especially Anglicans). The great Thomas Cranmer, one of our leading lights and primary architect of the *Book of Common Prayer*, suffered for the gospel. But maybe we're tempted to think he was somehow superhuman, on a different level to us? He wasn't. In March 2006, at a service to commemorate the 450th anniversary of Cranmer's martyrdom, the Archbishop of Canterbury, Rowan Williams, said, quite rightly, that Cranmer was 'a constitutionally timid man struggling to be brave (and all the braver for that).' He was an urbane, scholarly man by temperament, not a fighter.

We see that of course in the story of how Cranmer recanted under pressure from his inquisitors while in prison. But then his superb final act, placing the right hand which signed the recantation of his Protestant faith into that fire on Broad Street in Oxford—'forasmuch as my hand offended in writing contrary to my heart, therefore my hand shall first be punished.'

My old church history teacher, Rudi Heinze, pointed out in his own commemoration lecture on Cranmer how important it is to note that God chose *this* man for martyrdom—not Calvin, not Luther. They would have made great martyrs. I wouldn't mind reading their last words and hearing about the blaze of glory with which they departed! What stirring words they would have been! Speeches to make Martin Luther King's pale into insignificance!

Yet they died in their beds. And God chose a man constitutionally least able to be a martyr to be a martyr. Why? Because His power is made perfect in weakness, and by His Spirit He can sustain and strengthen even the most 'constitutionally timid,' like Thomas Cranmer.

Paul's words here in 2 Timothy are not a senseless call to martyrdom. Paul gives Timothy more than adequate reasons for joining him, and the Lord Himself, in suffering for the gospel, whatever form that suffering might have taken. He gives him a reminder of the gospel itself.

## It's worth it for the gospel

He's basically saying in verses 9 and 10 that it's worth it for the gospel. These verses are meant to motivate us as we unashamedly stand firm. Yes, it involves persecution, hard work, standing out. But the gospel is a more than adequate compensation.

So finally, let's just have a look at how Paul reminds Timothy of the gospel. It starts in verse 9. 'God saved us and called us to a holy calling, not because of our works but because of his own purpose and grace.' The gospel is first of all about being *saved*. It says we need saving—from our sin, from the wrath of God against our sin, and from sin's destructive effects and consequences. As Paul says in 1 Thessalonians chapter 1, Jesus rescued us from the wrath to come. And 'God has not destined us for wrath, but to obtain salvation through our Lord Jesus Christ, who died for us' (1 Thess. 5:9-10).

The gospel says that only happens by *grace*. He saved us 'not because of our works but because of his own purpose and grace.' We can't do it ourselves, or play a part in our own salvation. God needs to do it. And He does do it—yet not, according to verse 9, because of our good works—but simply because He is gracious and kind.

What a motivation for Timothy! He might feel quite guilty after these opening paragraphs. He may have failed in the past unashamedly to stand for Jesus in some situation or other. We all have, haven't we? None of us has always been as bold as we should have been. And so Paul reminds us here that God relates to us on the basis of grace. He's a gracious and forgiving God who doesn't save us because we're so worthy—but in spite of the fact that we're not.

So what a motivation for us to share in suffering for the gospel. It's a great gospel! But I wonder if such grace can also sometimes be a cause for embarrassment? Because there are plenty of preachers who try to water down God's grace, by adding things to it. They were around in Timothy's day, adding circumcision or food laws or religious festivals and experiences to the requirements for being saved. And they're around today too, insisting that God only helps those who help themselves, or God won't save you unless you do this or that or something else.

Historically the message that God saves us entirely without reference to our good works has been something which people *have* shied away from. Because the radical free grace of God can appear just too good to be true. So this reminder of it here is not only a great motivation for Timothy, it's also a reminder not to water down the message.

And then Paul goes on to highlight at the end of verse 9 another aspect of the gospel which will motivate Timothy. God saved us because of His grace which He gave us, 'in Christ Jesus before the ages began.' Now there's a fabulous truth to get our minds around. If Paul has so far been appealing to Timothy's recent history and heritage as a way of encouraging him, then what about appealing to the plan of God from eternity past? God decided to save us even before He created the universe.

Again, that's a slightly double-edged reminder isn't it? Because not only will the truth of God's predestination encourage and spur Timothy on, it might also be a cause of trouble for him. Because there's no end of people, even Christians and theologians, who are ready to deny that God has such decisive control over things. It's not a popular truth, predestination. So if we're tempted to be ashamed of it or to downplay it, Paul reminds us here that if we do we're downplaying a key element of the gospel itself.

But finally, let's just note one other aspect of the gospel which Paul highlights in verse 10 to motivate Timothy. Clearly the whole plan of salvation focuses on Christ Jesus, who's mentioned twice in verses 9 and 10. The gospel is after all the testimony about Him. What has He done? Well, verse 10: in His appearing, His life and death, He has—hear those stunning words—'abolished death and brought life and immortality to light through the gospel.'

If death is defeated and immortality has been won for us as Christians, then what does it matter if we have to suffer for a little while? There may be pain and difficulty in being Christian—that's par for the course when we follow a crucified Lord and proclaim an unpopular gospel. But it's worth it in the end. As the great hymn puts it: 'to everyone who conquers, a crown of life shall be; we with the King of glory, shall reign eternally.'[2]

Eternal life is on offer, and at stake. Again, some will mock the very idea. They will scoff at the thought of a crucified Jesus who comes back to life three days later and promises a resurrection just like that to all His followers. That sounded as fanciful to Timothy's congregation as it sometimes does to us. Richard Dawkins once dismissed it as 'so petty, so trivial, so local, so earth-bound, so unworthy of the universe.'[3]

But don't be ashamed of the gospel, and least of all the resurrection, because it's *true*. It's all true. It's not just a fairy tale or a game or a way to make a living. It's the sure hope of life and immortality for all who trust in Jesus, guaranteed by the solid reality of His own resurrection from the dead.

You can hear Paul getting excited about it in these verses. Don't be ashamed Timothy! Because God has saved *us*, you and me. He's called *us*, not because of our works but because of His grace. *Our* saviour has appeared, Timothy! 'He died eternal life to bring, and lives that death may die.'[4] So keep going my friend, my brother, my beloved child.

These are words for us too, to encourage each other with. Be faithful to our spiritual heritage. Let's suffer together without shame. Because it's worth it for the gospel.

---

2. 'Stand Up, Stand Up for Jesus' by George Duffield, Jr. (1818–88).

3. https://www.youtube.com/watch?v=zF5bPI92-5o

4. 'Crown him with many crowns' by Matthew Bridges (1851).

# 2

# Unashamedly Standing by Paul

## *2 Timothy 1:8-18*

Since 2 Timothy is probably Paul's last letter, it's a letter which is looking to the future and the handing on of the baton, as it were. He wants Timothy to take over and continue what he's been doing. But, more immediately, Paul wants Timothy to come to see him in prison. So in chapter 4 verse 9 he says plainly: 'Do your best to come to me soon,' and in verse 21, 'Do your best to come before winter.' Now that's because he wants his cloak back before it gets too cold. But it's also because he doesn't want Timothy to back away from him. The letter is a call to loyalty: loyalty to the gospel—yes—but also loyalty to Paul himself.

In the previous chapter we looked at what I said was a key verse in the letter. 2 Timothy 1:8 says, 'Do not be ashamed of the testimony about our Lord, nor of me his prisoner, but share in suffering for the gospel by the power of God.' And we looked at the idea of being ashamed of the gospel, ashamed of Jesus. We saw how we might be tempted to be ashamed of the gospel because it's the message of a crucified Messiah—and crucifixion was not a very popular thing to have happen to you in those days. We saw how the testimony about Jesus was outlined in verses 9 and 10. It's a message of free grace, to predestined people, who are heading for immortality in heaven. And we thought a bit about how that would sound laughable to people, and hence be a potential cause of embarrassment. But in this chapter, we're going to unpack the rest of verse 8 and the rest of the first chapter of this letter. And that means looking at this command not to be ashamed of Paul.

That's something of a startling idea at first isn't it? Jesus, after all, was the Messiah—the Son of God Himself. You can see why loyalty to Him was important. But Paul was just a man. How dare he place himself next to Jesus and the gospel and demand that Timothy show him loyalty too? And does that mean he expects *us* to stand by him too?

Well, we need to start by considering what the situation is for Paul. We know already from verse 8 that he's a prisoner. Why is he in jail? After reminding Timothy of the gospel in verses 9 and 10, he says for this gospel 'I was appointed a preacher and apostle and teacher—which is why I suffer as I do' (verses 11-12).

He's suffering because he teaches the gospel. Some people didn't like what he was preaching, and had ganged up on him. When he was beaten up by a mob in Jerusalem, he was arrested. Currently he's languishing in a cell, awaiting trial on trumped up charges. And as the trial wore on, his friends deserted him. So he tells us in chapter 4 verse 16, 'At my first defence no one came to stand by me, but all deserted me.' He was abandoned, with no character witnesses to speak up in his defence, no friends to support and pray for him. No Christian Concern lawyer at his side or sympathetic bloggers making his case in the public arena for him.

So he says in chapter 1 verse 15—'You are aware that all who are in Asia turned away from me, among whom are Phygelus and Hermogenes.' It sounds like a massive overstatement doesn't it? Everyone in the province of Asia has deserted me. But it was true. No one had leapt to his defence. Even Phygelus and Hermogenes. They're not mentioned anywhere else, so I don't know who they were. But Timothy knew them. They must have been former friends, maybe even colleagues in the ministry. It must have hurt to write their names next to the words 'deserted me.'

Timothy would have been very disappointed to hear this. 'Even *Phygelus!'*

How had it come to this? 'Don't be ashamed of the testimony about our Lord, nor of me his prisoner.' Surely if there was one person he could count on it would be Timothy? But no, Paul senses that even Timothy might be tempted to distance himself from his spiritual father. But why be embarrassed by Paul?

## Embarrassed by Paul?

Well, I think there are several reasons why people might be tempted to be embarrassed by Paul. For a start it's because of his status. Don't be ashamed of me, his *prisoner*, writes Paul. Yes, Paul is in prison. Not a nice open prison in the Home Counties but a dirty, stinking, dark, difficult to find, Roman prison. Being chained up in an unhygienic, rat-infested cell drove many to suicide, as they were abandoned by their families out of shame or fear.

### Paul's status

Paul and Timothy lived in a society obsessed with status, which had a powerful code of shame and honour. And once you were branded a criminal you were bottom of the heap, and would find it very difficult to rise again to a higher status. If all this sounds distant to us, in his excellent commentary on 2 Timothy, Chris Green warns us that this concept of status has a very contemporary application. For,

> the same patterns and dangers are easily visible in our society, and in our churches today. Some congregations have a higher status than others, whether because of their size (small defers to large), resources (poor defers to wealthy) or membership (older defers to younger, especially if the younger are students). Of course, no-one would ever refer to 'high status churches' because that would be too crude; the term we use instead is 'strategic.'[1]

---

1. Chris Green, *Finishing the Race: Reading 2 Timothy Today* (Sydney: Aquila Press, 2000), p. 52.

I used that quote in a church I once worked in, and there was an audible gasp, a sharp intake of breath, as we all recognized ourselves in this description. Chris Green goes on to say that, 'Paul found himself in a low-status position, in a deeply status driven culture. Prison... was a place of dishonour and shame. It was, to their eyes, definitely not strategic.'[2]

To polite Roman society that was the end of Paul. And in the eyes of many if not most *church* people, that was the end of Paul. So why should Timothy be ashamed of Paul? Well, because everybody else was. At the church growth conference or the EMA (the Ephesian Ministry Assembly) of A.D. 63, people come up to Timothy... 'You're not still sticking with that loser Paul, are you? You know he's a bit passé since that little incident with the riot and the arrest and everything. If you want to get ahead in ministry these days it's best to forget about Paul, and his funny little ways. We've got a seminar on new methods of church growth this afternoon, with a great speaker from a big, thriving church...'

Tempted to be ashamed about Paul the prisoner, and embarrassed about being associated with him? You bet.

You may remember that in the last chapter I said I'd written to a dozen of my contemporaries from theological college, to ask if they were ever ashamed of the gospel or of Paul. Well, one minister friend wrote about this issue of status. His temptation? 'I want to appear successful,' he writes, 'be respected by other evangelical ministers, have people praise things I've done, have the sort of ministry that gets a good write up in *Evangelicals Now*. I *don't* want to serve God unrecognized in difficulty and obscurity.'

He's honest. That's a temptation for every minister. But the fact is, if the Apostle Paul, the greatest theologian and missionary of the past 2000 years, could serve God in a shameful prison cell, then we don't need to have an

---

2. Green, *Finishing the Race*, p. 52.

international ministry or be in a big strategic church in order to be significant and useful in God's eyes.

Paul knew difficulty and obscurity and opposition. Elsewhere in the Bible we hear that some thought he was an unimpressive preacher, a weedy little man with laughably little skill as an orator (see 2 Cor. 10:10). But here we are, all gathered around a short letter he wrote, trying to understand every last detail. It just goes to show how wrong a worldly perspective can be. A worldly perspective would deploy the great theologian to the big church. Yet God puts him in prison.

That might be why Phygelus and Hermogenes had deserted Paul. It was certainly part of the reason why others left. In chapter 4 verse 10 Paul says, 'Demas, in love with this present world has deserted me and gone to Thessalonica, Crescens to Galatia, Titus to Dalmatia.' It doesn't say these men have abandoned the ministry, or stopped believing in Jesus. But they've abandoned Paul. Demas for worldly reasons; the others too I think.

Of course many never even consider Christian ministry for the same worldly reasons of status. Why demean themselves or voluntarily slip down the ladder of social acceptability? Why take up Christian leadership as the church dwindles in importance? Better to carry on with a job your mum would be proud of, than to give it all up for the kind of low-status ministry advocated by Paul. People are ashamed because of status.

This sort of thing could put some people off entering ministry—the fact that if you are a complementarian, or orthodox on sexuality, for example, you may never be allowed to exercise ministry at a senior level in the Church of England. Career minded clergy would be seriously dissuaded from joining up on such terms. But what would Paul say to that...?

## Paul's doctrine

Another reason Timothy might be tempted to be ashamed of Paul has to do with what he taught. People are ashamed of Paul because of his doctrine. We've already considered how some people might find his gospel in verses 9 and 10 somewhat embarrassing. It can sound bizarre, or strange, or too good to be true. And the fact that Paul urges Timothy in verse 13 not to depart from the pattern of teaching he learned from Paul also shows that this was a prime reason why some people were deserting him: they didn't like what he taught.

But it's also just obvious that people don't like Paul's doctrine. All my friends said this when I emailed them. 'It seems to me,' wrote one, 'that Christians can be ashamed of Paul because he's perceived by some to be a sexist or against women.' 'It's interesting,' writes another, 'how Paul has always been the sticking point and still is.' He admits to being somewhat apologetic about Paul's teaching on marriage, for instance, because he fears what people will think of him.

Another pastor in a middle-of-the-road church somewhere in the North of England writes: 'Out here in the hinterland almost everyone is embarrassed by Paul and his message. We much prefer to speak about the gospel being the words of *Jesus*. Being Pauline [*of Paul*] is an insult rather than a good thing.' He goes on, 'As such it's tempting for me to say—"hmmm yes Paul did get carried away... He is fearsome at times..." His ethics particularly are reviled in our church.'

To say that—'we like Jesus, but not Paul'—is particularly common. Jesus, of course, was gentle and mild, but Paul was harsh and judgmental—so we're told. Jesus never said anything controversial, apparently; it's Paul who makes all the politically incorrect comments. So let's say we're 'Jesus Christians,' and leave it at that, shall we? Paul? Oh, he's interesting but not to be taken too seriously.

Whether it's what Paul said about homosexuality, or what he says about women, or what he says about marriage, or what he writes about the cross or judgment or church discipline… it's tempting, and would perhaps be extremely convenient in our ecclesiastical context, to simply forget about Paul.

A godly, gentle, family man who pastors another middle-of-the-road Anglican church says: 'When, in the space of two months, the churchwarden, resident retired clergyman, and organist all independently resign because of the message that is being preached… and when you look at your children and see their confusion that someone wants to shout at their Daddy on a Sunday morning, and when you know that a small change in the message is all that is needed to make all the trouble disappear, then, I tell you, you're tempted to water down, to shy away, from what the Bible says, especially Paul.'

Why does he not shy away from it then? He writes: 'God has told me two things that help me stand fast: first, that like it or not, life and immortality are only found in the gospel of Jesus. And second, that to face trouble for preaching the gospel is nothing unusual at all.' And that's exactly what the Apostle Paul is saying to Timothy as well. So in chapter 1 verse 12 Paul says, despite what I'm going through because of the gospel, 'I am not ashamed, for I know whom I have believed, and I am convinced that he is able to guard until that day what has been entrusted to me.'

Paul endures suffering because he knows Jesus. As my friend put it, he knows that life and immortality are only found in the gospel of Jesus. And he's convinced of His power and presence in the midst of hardship. What is it Jesus is guarding in that verse? Literally it says Jesus can guard 'my deposit.' In verse 14 the same word, 'deposit' is used of the gospel itself, which Timothy is to guard. It's used that way at the end of 1 Timothy 6, verse 20 too: 'O Timothy, guard the deposit entrusted to you.'

So it probably means Jesus guards Paul's gospel, his doctrine. But it might also, in verse 12 at least, refer to what Paul has entrusted to Jesus—that is, his life, and his eternal security. It can be read that way as well, as the footnote in some Bibles indicates. Paul knows and trusts his saviour, and is confident as he waits for 'that day,' the day of judgment and reward. Like it or not, only Paul's gospel will be of any use to us on that day.

### Paul's tactics

So Timothy might be tempted to be ashamed of Paul, because of his status, or because of his doctrine. But often the temptation to distance ourselves from Paul is more subtle than that. We might also be tempted to be ashamed of Paul's tactics.

Because that's partly why Paul is in prison in the first place. He went around preaching the gospel *openly*. He said things like 'gods made with hands are no gods at all.' That wasn't very sensitive in a place like Ephesus where Timothy was, for instance, where there was a thriving trade in silver statues of the goddess Artemis. And what happened in Ephesus? There was a riot against Paul and the Christians (see Acts 19). So people say, 'Look—this gospel of Jesus brings trouble. Its preachers are clearly disturbers of the peace.'

Part of the purpose of the book of Acts is to show that the trouble originates with those who feel threatened by the gospel. *They* start the riots, not Christians. But the false accusations might well stick. You can imagine people saying, 'Well, you know, Paul's tactics *were* a bit "confrontational"... Perhaps he *could* have been more subtle. He should have stopped the Ephesians, for instance, from burning all their magic scrolls and throwing away their idols so publicly. Why not do it privately, quietly, rather than trying to make a public point?'

Often we do have legitimate differences about tactics when it comes to working for the gospel. Some good orthodox people will do it one way, while others choose a different approach. Same message, different tactics.

Recently there was the story of Harry Hammond, a sixty-nine-year-old pensioner, who was attacked in the street by young people, ended up flat on his back in the middle of the street, had clods of earth thrown at him, and water poured on him. Who was arrested for causing a public disturbance? *He* was. You might think it strange that the man assaulted was arrested, rather than the people who attacked him. But Harry Hammond was a Christian, an open-air evangelist. And that day he held in his hands a poster which said 'Stop Immorality. Stop Homosexuality. Jesus is Lord.'

Now I'm not a placard-waving sort of person. So by nature the first thing I want to do when I hear that story is say, 'Oh, I wouldn't do that. That's too provocative.' But it would be a short step from there to saying he had it coming. And to do that would be to side with Harry Hammond's attackers.

I instinctively want to distance myself from people I might label extremists. Don't you? So if a church organization or group appears to me to be 'too right-wing' or too strident or not sophisticated enough, my instinct is to shy away from it. I might say bad things about that society, so that people don't associate them with me, and so I can appear more balanced, measured, moderate, 'mainstream.'

There are various evangelical leaders who've been out of favour with the Church of England authorities in the last few years. Fine gospel preachers. But some of us might not like the tactics they use, or not get on with them personally, or think they might have avoided trouble if only they'd done it differently or not been so harsh. So we're tempted to distance ourselves from people who preach the same gospel. As another friend of mine writes, 'I want a quiet life… and don't want anything to disturb it. I want to be liked.' Don't we all! So, he continues: 'I'm embarrassed about association with anyone too fanatical, e.g. Paul.' I think Timothy could have empathized with that—maybe he was tempted to be embarrassed by his 'fanatical' friend too.

Have you heard of Archbishop Akinola from Nigeria? An orthodox bishop who did a great deal to guard the gospel and refute error. He wrote something in the *Church Times* a few years ago about issues in the Anglican Communion. I agree with him theologically on those issues. But some of the ways he phrased his views made my toes curl in embarrassment. I could sense that other *Church Times* readers would simply hate what he was saying. So, I confess, it's tempting to distance myself from Nigeria, even though we're on the same wavelength theologically.

Maybe for you it's not Archbishop Akinola or Harry Hammond. Maybe it's a Christian in your office who's a bit outspoken. Do you know someone like that? Someone who's a Christian, but of whom you're, well, a bit embarrassed? There are many Christians who are 'not quite of our type' but who are standing up for Jesus, and Paul, and the gospel. They may not do it the way we would do it, so it's tempting to say, 'I'm not like that. I'm not one of them.'

And I think that's what many people had done with Paul. They'd deserted him, and pretended not to know him because it was too uncomfortable. And *he* wasn't just an ordinary Christian or an ordinary minister or bishop either. He was an apostle of Jesus Christ, by the will of God. A specially commissioned messenger of the Lord of Time and Space. And yet still they deserted him.

Except one man hadn't done that. In chapter 1 verses 16, 17 and 18 we hear about Onesiphorus. He 'often refreshed me,' says Paul. Onesiphorus provided Paul with much-needed sustenance, because there were no prison canteens in Rome. And Onesiphorus didn't mind that Paul was of low status. He was probably a businessman of some kind, moving between Ephesus and Rome. And when he was in Rome on business, he 'was not ashamed of my chains' writes Paul. He wasn't ashamed of being seen with the prisoner. He didn't mind that to embrace Paul was to share his squalor and face the same rejection from the world and from a worldly church. Verse 17 tells us he searched for Paul, 'earnestly,' keenly, so that he might be as supportive of him in suffering as he was before in Ephesus.

Why is Paul mentioning Onesiphorus? Is it just to pray that Onesiphorus would be blessed by God? I think there's more to it than that, don't you? Notice that key word 'ashamed' again in verse 16. Chapter 1 verse 8 says we must not be ashamed of the gospel or of Paul. Paul himself is not ashamed of the gospel, verse 12. And Onesiphorus is a prime example of what it looks like to not be ashamed of Paul. As such, Onesiphorus is the model for Timothy to follow. When he gets to Rome, *he* should seek out Paul, and unashamedly stand by him too.

But what can we do? Paul's imprisonment ended many years ago. By all accounts he ended his life a martyr, beheaded for the Word of God and the testimony of Jesus Christ. How can we show loyalty to him now, across the centuries? Or is there nothing we can do to apply this passage today?

## Guarding Paul's gospel

I think the application for us is found in verses 13 and 14. We stand by Paul if we follow and guard his gospel. 'Follow the pattern of the sound words that you have heard from me, in the faith and love that are in Christ Jesus. By the Holy Spirit who dwells within us, guard the good deposit entrusted to you.'

Standing by Paul means following the gospel as he taught it. His teaching, as we have it recorded in Acts and his letters, provides us with a model, a pattern, to follow. That's why God gave him to us as the apostle to the Gentiles. So we can follow Paul's gospel, his sound words. That word, 'sound' in verse 13 just means 'healthy.' Paul's gospel brings health and life, vitality and vigour to the churches that follow it.

Where there is death and stagnation, decline and despair, what's needed is not some trendy updated gospel that's more appealing to modern people. What's needed when churches are dying is the pattern of sound, healthy, life-giving words which Timothy heard from Paul and we read of here. So we need not only to follow Paul's gospel, but also to guard it. In a church or denomination torn apart by schisms and distressed by heresy we need more of Paul, not less.

We must guard his gospel, which was entrusted to Timothy and then through the ages entrusted to us. Because if we don't, the coming generations will not have a healthy spiritual diet. What will happen to their churches if they only know a mangled, diseased, corrupted version of the good news of Jesus Christ? It will poison churches, ruin fellowships, and stunt evangelism. Someone once said:

> If I profess with the loudest voice and clearest exposition every portion of the truth of God except precisely that little point that the world and the devil are at the moment attacking, I am not confessing Christ.... Where the battle rages is where the loyalty of the soldier is proved, and to be steady on all the battlefield besides is merely flight and disgrace if he flinches at that point.[3]

I think that's right. It won't make us popular, but I think that means we need to guard the gospel and its implications in debates that are not at the heart of the gospel, but where the Bible's teaching is currently under severe attack.

So we need to follow and guard Paul's health-giving words. Those words may also bring *suffering*, but we know for sure that Jesus is able to look after us. There's a reason Paul keeps mentioning 'that day' in verse 12 and verse 18 for instance. It's to remind us that any suffering for the gospel now is nothing in the light of the eternal reward for those who persevere.

So if you want to be like Onesiphorus in our day, follow Paul's gospel and guard it too. We can only do this, of

---

3.   This rousing quote is from a novel by Elizabeth Rundle Charles, *The Chronicles of the Schönberg-Cotta Family* (Thomas Nelson, 1864). It is not, as is often claimed, from Martin Luther.

course, with the help of God Himself. 'By the Holy Spirit who dwells within us, guard the good deposit....' He may have entrusted the good deposit to us, but that doesn't mean God has taken His own hands off it. His Spirit energizes and empowers us to keep and guard the gospel.

Only with His help can we spot new threats to it, theologically or philosophically or pastorally. Only He can strengthen us to withstand the inevitable assaults of criticism and rejection that come when we follow Jesus and are loyal to His apostles. So let's pray for one another, that all of us would stand by Paul.

# 3

# Soldiers of Christ
## 2 Timothy 2:1-13

Straight after I was baptized on 8th October 1972, the minister made the sign of the cross on my head. He told the congregation (in the words of the 1662 *Book of Common Prayer*) that he was doing this 'in token that hereafter he shall not be ashamed to confess the faith of Christ crucified, and manfully to fight under his banner against sin, the world, and the devil, and to continue Christ's faithful soldier and servant unto his life's end.' So I was publicly conscripted into a spiritual battle at an early age. I confirmed my willingness to be part of it as a teenager, and voluntarily took oaths to undertake leadership responsibilities in it as others laid their hands on my head at ordination. So as an ordained minister in the Church of England, I guess there's no way to escape it. I must fight valiantly and contend for the faith! The alternative is to be a 'pagan,' a word which was originally military slang for a non-combatant.[1]

Paul tells Timothy in this passage to be 'a good solider of Christ Jesus.' What does that mean, as a description of a gospel minister? Am I to physically threaten and wrestle people into church? That would be toxic masculinity and muscular Christianity at its worst! And what does Paul

---

1.  See Diarmaid MacCulloch, *A History of Christianity: The First Three Thousand Years* (London: Allen Lane, 2009), p. 156. cf. Lee Gatiss, *Fight Valiantly: Contending for the Faith against False Teaching in the Church* (London: Lost Coin, 2022), p. 8.

mean in this passage about recruiting reliable, trustworthy people to pass the gospel on to?

## Solemn succession

The first thing Paul talks about here is solemn succession in gospel ministry. So look again with me at verses 1 and 2:

> You then, my child, be strengthened by the grace that is in Christ Jesus, and what you have heard from me in the presence of many witnesses entrust to faithful men who will be able to teach others also.

Paul urges Timothy to be strong, strengthened by grace. Grace saves us—we were saved not by our works but because of God's own purpose and grace which He gave us in Christ Jesus, says chapter 1 verse 9. But the grace that saves us is also the motivation, the driving force, which strengthens us for Christian life and ministry.

But why do we need to be continually strengthened and impelled by grace? Well, because God did not give us a spirit of cowardice, or fear, but a spirit of *power*, of love and of self-control (1:7). We need power, strength from God, in order to share in suffering for the gospel (1:8). Paul himself is suffering as he writes this letter of course, languishing in jail because of his public preaching of the gospel.

Timothy also needs to be strengthened in his resolve. There is a battle going on for his soul, and for the heart of his ministry. This letter is a call to loyalty, a call to be loyal to Christ and loyal to Paul His holy apostle—in a context where to flinch or compromise and just back off from these things a little would be all that's needed to make many of the difficulties fade away.

Phygelus and Hermogenes at the end of chapter 1 have turned away and gone a different route in their ministries. Onesiphorus, on the other hand, has not. He was loyal to Paul, searched him out and stood by him. And that's what Paul wants his younger co-worker Timothy to do too. He expects better from Timothy. Which is why he starts chapter

2 with 'You then, *my child...*' 'You're different. You're mine, Timothy, my close companion, my co-worker, part of my mission agency team. And here's what I need you to do.'

### Bishop Timothy

What's he to do? Well, he's already told him what to do, of course, in chapter 1. Follow the pattern of sound, healthy words that you heard from me (1:13), and guard the good deposit (1:14). And here in chapter 2 he tells him one way to do that. 'Those words you heard from me, in the presence of many witnesses, entrust them in turn to other faithful folk who will be able to pass them on.'[2]

Paul is concerned about succession in gospel ministry. He wants the gospel to continue in Ephesus (where Timothy is currently ministering), even when Timothy himself comes to see Paul in Rome. It may be a temporary thing, just while Timothy is away. That's the immediate background context. But it sounds a little more than that to me. It sounds like Paul is telling him one important way that he can guard the good deposit *entrusted* to him is to *entrust* it in turn to others. You don't guard it by keeping it to yourself, but by sharing it and delivering it over to others.

It's a bit like Timothy is a bishop. Indeed, many Reformation-era commentators called him just that.[3] Why? Because that's what his ministry looked like. In 1 Timothy, Paul tells him to keep other teachers in Ephesus in line, and command them not to teach various heresies (1 Tim. 1:3, 18). He tells him the kind of people who should be appointed as elders and overseers in the church

---

2.   Incidentally, although the ESV here says 'faithful men,' the Greek noun is from the generic word *anthrōpos*, not the more specific word for a male person, *anēr*. So the NIV is probably right to translate it 'reliable *people*,' so as not to give some the mistaken impression that 2 Timothy 2:2 is explicitly taking sides in the complementarian-egalitarian debate. However, in 1 Timothy 6:11, Paul does use *anthrōpos* to refer to Timothy himself (cf. 2 Timothy 3:17) so the absence of the more specific word for males does not necessarily mean he has both men and women in mind either.

3.   See Gatiss and Green (eds.), *1-2 Thessalonians, 1-2 Timothy, Titus, Philemon*, pp. lv, 110–14.

31

(1 Tim. 3:1-13), presumably because he was to have a hand in such ordination and appointments. He told him how to organize things in the church. And just as Timothy himself was set aside by the council of elders, by the laying on of hands (1 Tim. 4:14), he is told that he should not be hasty in the laying on of hands (1 Tim. 5:22), in ordaining others. And when it comes to other elders in Ephesus, Timothy is to keep an eye on their pay, their stipends (1 Tim. 5:17), hear charges against elders, and rebuke their behaviour where necessary (1 Tim. 5:19-20). These are what we might call episcopal functions. So as John Mayer (1583–1664) commented, 'it is not to be doubted but that he sat in Ephesus as chief of the bishops, as all the ministers of the gospel were then called.'[4]

So this verse in 2 Timothy 2:2, is part of that picture. Timothy is not just some random young guy floating about in Ephesus wondering how he can serve the cause of truth in his day when suddenly, 'Oh look! A letter from Paul. I wonder what he says I should do.' No, he's been training alongside Paul for a few years, serving as an apprentice, doing ministry; and now he's been given an important ministry in the strategic city of Ephesus—a ministry that involves training, appointing and overseeing the ministry of other elders.

And Paul wants to make sure, as things start to look a bit dicey for him over in Rome, that this passing on of the gospel will continue even when Timothy leaves Asia and heads for Italy. After all, Timothy may not be going back.

### Public witnesses

In verse 2, Paul uses the phrase, 'in the presence of many witnesses.' This is an enigmatic little clause. Usually it is translated 'what you have heard from me in the presence of many witnesses [comma], entrust to faithful men' etc. That is, Paul's gospel is not some secret. It has been openly proclaimed. That's why he's in such trouble of course. But there are lots of people who know what he stands for and

---

4.   Gatiss and Green (eds.), *1-2 Thessalonians, 1-2 Timothy, Titus, Philemon*, p. 112.

what his doctrine is. Many are witnesses to Paul's way of speaking and doing things. So, Timothy, you and these other guys know what I taught. That's what you are to pass on.

And it's a good thing for a church, or a denomination, to have publicly available accounts of its teaching. We are not to be one of those esoteric, gnostic sects, keeping our secret doctrines to ourselves and only giving them out to the initiated few. No, our confession of faith is on public record. Everyone knows what we profess to believe, and we can be held accountable to it. Legally, in the Church of England, for example, that public standard of faith is defined in canon law. So Canon A5 states that:

> The doctrine of the Church of England is grounded in the Holy Scriptures, and in such teachings of the ancient Fathers and Councils of the Church as are agreeable to the said Scriptures. In particular such doctrine is to be found in the Thirty-nine Articles of Religion, The Book of Common Prayer, and the Ordinal.

This faith has been passed down to us, before many witnesses. And it is that which those of us who are ordained have voluntarily chosen to commit ourselves to, publicly. We affirmed that the Church of England 'has *borne witness* to Christian truth in its historic formularies, the Thirty-nine Articles of Religion, The Book of Common Prayer and the Ordering of Bishops, Priests and Deacons.' And in a declaration, we were asked to publicly 'affirm your loyalty to this inheritance of faith as your inspiration and guidance under God' (Canon C15).

I think that is right and proper. What you heard from me, in the presence of many *witnesses*... That apostolic doctrine, publicly confessed and publicly accessible in our official formularies. Though I sometimes wonder whether we could read these words in 2 Timothy 2:2 slightly differently. Put the comma after 'heard from me,' instead. So it reads, 'what you heard from me [comma], in the presence of many witnesses entrust to faithful men…' That is, 'what you heard me say, entrust to others—and do it publicly.'

The commas in our modern translations are not an inspired part of the original. Read this way, what Paul is saying is that this is *all* to be done publicly: the faith and the passing on. Which is in keeping with the purpose of this letter itself, of course. This letter, ostensibly to Timothy as an individual, is probably to be read out to the whole congregation—the 'Grace be with *you*' at the very end of chapter 4 is a plural 'you.' I think Paul expected the congregation to read this letter over Timothy's shoulder, so to speak. And of course, *we* have this letter now too.

Wherever we put the comma, the public witnessing of the truth of the gospel is important here. So Paul is saying, pass on these instructions, and the gospel—and let as many people as possible know that I said so! And let it be known by as many as possible that these people you hand the gospel on to have been entrusted with something vital, that they have a public trust to keep hold of, and that they can't therefore wriggle out of. As Richard Hooker (1554–1600) said, being ordained and entrusted with the gospel like this is a solemn and public thing, and people who have had something entrusted to them like this can't 'put it off and on like a cloak as the weather serves.'[5] The public witnessing of this handing on of the baton is an important part of ensuring people take the commitment to it seriously.

Certainly the Church of England also thinks that 'all things should be done decently and in order' (1 Cor. 14:40). As Article 23 says:

> It is not lawful for any man to take upon him the office of public preaching, or ministering the Sacraments in the Congregation, before he be lawfully called, and sent to execute the same. And those we ought to judge lawfully called and sent, which be chosen and called to this work

---

5. Richard Hooker, *Of the Laws of Ecclesiastical Polity: A Critical Edition with Modern Spelling* (3 vols. edited by Arthur Stephen McGrade; Oxford: Oxford University Press, 2013), 2:285 (5.77.1).

by men who have public authority given unto them in the Congregation, to call and send Ministers into the Lord's vineyard.

## Reliability

So there is a solemn trust here, to be passed on carefully for the future flourishing of the gospel. But to whom is this solemn succession to be given? Obviously the other Pastoral Epistles (1 Timothy and Titus) lay out the qualifications in more detail, as well as other parts of the New Testament that teach us about biblical patterns of ministry (such as 1 Cor. 1–3, 2 Cor. 4, and 1 Pet. 5).

But Paul zeros in on two particular things here, to bear in mind when thinking about succession. The people we hand on to should be faithful, and they should be able to teach. They need both ability and reliability.

In terms of reliability or faithfulness, as Titus 1:9 says, they need to 'hold firm to the trustworthy word as taught.' You don't entrust something precious to people who have a less than firm grip. Imagine giving a diamond ring to such a person. The ring would end up down a sink. Imagine leaving your children with such a person. Would you be happy to see your kids helped across the road by someone with less than a firm grip? Similarly, we must hand on the baton of the gospel to people who have a firm grip on the gospel.

In the Bible, this firmness or 'faithfulness' is a vital characteristic for leaders. Because ultimately God Himself is a faithful God. He keeps His promises, His covenant. So to serve Him, we too must be faithful and true. We see this all over the Bible. Let me just select a few places where this emerges, to paint a picture of what Paul is getting at.

So, it was high praise for Moses when God said of him in Numbers 12 verse 7, 'He is *faithful* in all my house.' To be faithful in the Old Testament—the root is the same as the word 'Amen'—means to be loyal and trusty, established, sure, stable. God says in 1 Samuel 2:35 that He will raise up a *faithful* priest—and how does He define faithful? 'I will raise up for myself a faithful priest, who shall do according to what is in my heart and in my mind.' A faithful leader follows God closely.

When Nehemiah gives charge over Jerusalem to someone, in Nehemiah 7:2, he says it was because 'he was a more *faithful* and God-fearing man than many.' Nehemiah could trust him to do the job that needed doing, because this chap was faithful.

Faithfulness is also related to the truth. Proverbs 14:5, 'A *faithful* witness does not lie, but a false witness breathes out lies.' Faithfulness holds on to truth. And Proverbs 27:6, '*Faithful* are the wounds of a friend; profuse are the kisses of an enemy.' So faithfulness doesn't mean avoiding saying the hard things. It means sticking to truth, even if it hurts and is difficult.

And you may remember Daniel: 'the high officials and the satraps sought to find a ground for complaint against Daniel with regard to the kingdom, but they could find no ground for complaint or any fault, because he was *faithful*, and no error or fault was found in him' (Dan. 6:4). He was an honest, diligent man of integrity.

Jesus wondered 'Who then is the *faithful* and wise servant, whom his master has set over his household, to give them their food at the proper time?' (Matt. 24:45). That's a similar picture to when Paul says, 'it is required of stewards that they be found *faithful*' (1 Cor. 4:2). It's a word that conjures up a picture of a careful, industrious person in a position of responsibility. Similarly, Paul says elsewhere that you can tell someone will *not* be suitable as a pastor if they cannot manage the responsibility of managing their own household well (1 Tim. 3:4-5).

He calls Timothy 'my beloved and *faithful* child in the Lord' (1 Cor. 4:17) who was sent to Corinth specifically 'to remind you of my ways in Christ, as I teach them everywhere in every church.' You don't send as your representative someone who you don't trust to do things properly, and to conscientiously reflect your views, your teaching. And you don't send an untrustworthy person to carry your letters from one part of the ancient world to another. They might not get it there, or they might tamper with the letter, or they might misreport you or misinterpret you when asked about what you meant, for example. Which is why Paul specifically calls Tychicus, who delivered the Epistles of the Ephesians and Colossians to their destinations, 'a beloved brother and *faithful* minister in the Lord' (Eph. 6:21). He wanted to reassure the Ephesians that they could trust him as a letter carrier. Just as the nearby Colossians could trust Epaphras and Onesimus, whom Paul also calls 'faithful.' It was his stamp of approval and accreditation.

Peter does the same at the end of his first letter. He says, 'By Silvanus, a *faithful* brother as I regard him, I have written briefly to you, exhorting and declaring that this is the true grace of God. Stand firm in it' (1 Pet. 5:12). You can trust the guy who wrote down this letter for me (and who is possibly the one delivering it). He's faithful. I consider him reliable.

And Paul himself writes at the beginning of his first letter to Timothy, 'I thank him who has given me strength, Christ Jesus our Lord, because he judged me *faithful*, appointing me to his service' (1 Tim. 1:12).

So when Paul tells Timothy to entrust the teaching of the gospel to *faithful* folk, he doesn't just mean anybody who has faith. He's not just telling him to make sure they are believers. That should be taken as read. He means more than that. They need to be trustworthy and reliable people.

How can we know who is trustworthy and reliable to be entrusted with such a solemn responsibility? Well, Jesus gives us a hint in Luke 16.

> One who is faithful in a very little is also faithful in much, and one who is dishonest in a very little is also dishonest in much. If then you have not been faithful in the unrighteous wealth, who will entrust to you the true riches? And if you have not been faithful in that which is another's, who will give you that which is your own? (Luke 16:10-12)

This is why the process of becoming a minister can seem like a very long exercise. Why can't I just take over a church now?! Why all the training and apprenticeship and curacy?! Well, at its best, that is because we don't accelerate people into positions of significant leadership until they have shown that they can be trusted with that. And you only know if someone can be trusted with a big thing if they have proven it in a small thing. It's the same in the world. It's rare for someone to get a senior office of state without having had a smaller portfolio of responsibilities previously, and shown that they can be trusted with it. In businesses too, one usually needs to start at the bottom, prove your ability and reliability, before you take over as the CEO.

But if someone has been sacked from job after job in the secular world, and proved incompetent and untrustworthy with 'unrighteous wealth,' we don't just give them a job in the church 'because we're nice and like to give people a go.' The management of 'true riches' requires even more integrity, honesty and transparency than secular employment and political leadership. Which is why Paul elsewhere says that overseers ought not to be recent converts, but have a bit of a track record; and that they ought to have a reasonable reputation even with outsiders, non-believers (1 Tim. 3:6-7).

In the same way, if you can't trust someone to lead a small group Bible study, how can you trust them to be incumbent of a church? If they don't take it seriously when you ask them to lead a dorm on a summer camp, or do the prayers in an evening service, or give out service sheets at the door, how can you know they are future bishop material?

So don't balk at it if, when you are young, you are given less than stellar responsibilities in your church sometimes—if you have to clean a few toilets or help out in a Sunday school lesson or do some photocopying. These are opportunities to demonstrate and to grow in faithfulness.

A young guy once expressed to me how frustrated he was that if he 'went into the church' he wouldn't 'be allowed to be an incumbent of a church' for at least six or seven years. He'd have to do training and a curacy before that, he said with a sigh. Well, I can't remember what I said at the time, but I hope I said that that was an opportunity to grow in patience and in wisdom. And I hope I reminded him of Luke 12:48 and James 3:1, and that the greater responsibility we have, the more strictly we will be judged by God on the last day.

Since Christian ministry is about service, we can also say that if serving others is beneath you then leadership is beyond you. That could be a quote from someone. I saw it on the internet, not sure where now. But it's true isn't it? If serving others is beneath you then leadership in the church is not for you. Ministry is being a slave of Christ, not a ladder for personal fulfilment and earthly security. It's a vocation, not a profession. It requires faithfulness to Jesus and His message, not making up your own or gathering followers for yourself.

So Timothy is to entrust the gospel publicly to reliable people. It could sound a bit ordinary. We're not looking for stellar prospects, but steady eddies. We're not seeking potential superstars and religious celebrities who can stand out and bring in the crowds or manage a big budget. Just people who can be counted on. Though to be faithful to this calling in the midst of all the opposition you will face from the world, the flesh, and the devil is, in actual fact, a rather extraordinary feat.

### Ability

But these people are not just meant to be reliable. They are meant to be able to teach others also, says 2 Timothy 2:2. Ability and reliability go together.

What are they meant to teach? 2 Timothy 1:8 speaks about 'the testimony about our Lord.' But what is that? Paul reminds Timothy of it in verse 8 of this chapter too. 'Remember Jesus Christ,' he says in 2 Timothy 2:8, 'risen from the dead, the offspring of David, as preached in my gospel.'

Each word there is loaded, pregnant with meaning. And Timothy is to entrust the work in Ephesus to those who are able to unpack this, and teach it to others. And what they are to teach is also mentioned in chapter 3. They are to teach the Bible, which is utterly sufficient for life and ministry: 'All Scripture is breathed out by God and profitable *for teaching*, for reproof, for correction, and for training in righteousness, that *the man of God may be competent*, equipped for every good work' (2 Tim. 3:16-17). The 'man of God' there is the person we're talking about. It is not just a reference to every Christian, though obviously every Christian needs and loves the Bible. No, Paul uses it in 1 Timothy 6:11 to refer to Timothy himself and, as the footnote in the ESV says, it is a common Old Testament expression to describe a messenger of God.

So what he's saying is that as well as being a reliable character, these people need to know their Bibles and be able to handle them correctly. And not use other tools to go about their ministries. It's the Bible that is profitable for teaching. That's what makes us competent as Christian leaders, and equips us. Not the latest managerial techniques, however useful they may sometimes be. Not the potted wisdom of the ministry manuals, however applicable some of that might be.

But note that actually Paul doesn't say they should be able to teach the Bible. It's true that it's the Bible, the gospel, which they are meant to pass on. But the object of the verb 'to teach' here is not 'the Bible.' It's people. Other people. So my job is not done simply by regurgitating sound material from the pulpit each week. It's not faithful ministry if good theology goes from my library to their notebooks without actually engaging the hearts, minds and wills of the people.

You may have been taught (or you may have heard it said) that the way to grow a church is to 'just preach the Word!' This has led many of us into dead ends, not to mention relational difficulties with the people we are called to actually pastor. I sometimes speak to clergy friends, and when I ask them how church is going, how it was on Sunday, they tell me all about the great sermon they preached. Now in one way, I can understand that. We're preachers, so we talk about what we've been preaching. But I asked about church, and church is more than just my personal lecture theatre where I get to deliver scintillating homilies each week. Church is the people. We're meant to teach the Bible... to people.

So that means understanding people. More specifically, understanding the people in front of me each Sunday as I preach my scintillating sermon. I may 'get the Word right,' but fail properly to exegete my audience. And the clunking mismatch, as I speak over them, or down to them, or below them, or entirely tangential to them, can be jarring. We're not being faithful pastors if we just download sound teaching into the pulpit microphone and onto the church website each week, unless it is also sticking in the souls of our people somehow.

So I have to know the people, and love the people enough to make it possible for them to hear what I'm trying to teach. To seduce them with the Word means more than just setting it out nicely on a Sunday. It means my life and conversation and personal relationships do come into my ability to teach, even more than my rhetorical skill and knowledge of Greek participles.

'Entrust the gospel to faithful men who will be able to teach others also.' Now, Paul may mean here that Timothy is to find people who will be able to teach the congregation when he's not there. But it could also be about passing it on to others who can pass it on to others. That is, train pastors who can train pastors. After all, say John Richardson and Dub Gannon,

> although Jesus preached to hundreds and even thousands, his focus was on just twelve disciples. Yet it was through these disciples that the gospel was established and proclaimed after his death and resurrection. In a similar way, a pastor who trains a dozen other effective pastors

41

may, in the end, ensure the pastoring of far more people overall than pastors who preach sermons to hundreds but train no leaders to succeed them.[6]

This is true apostolic succession. Not some tactile laying on of hands, but a succession of true, faithful teaching. What counts is the faithfulness with which we communicate the gospel to the next generation, not whether we have been touched by someone who was touched by a bishop who was touched by a patriarch who was (somewhere down the line) ordained by Jesus.

We've already seen how succession works, in this letter. In chapter 1, Paul wrote about his own ancestors, who served God with a clear conscience (2 Tim. 1:3). And he spoke about Timothy's grandmother and mother, who also believed and passed on the teaching of the Bible to Timothy (1:5-6, 2 Tim. 3:15). So Paul and Timothy are both the fruit of successful doctrinal succession, in a sense.

But it's not just meant to work in families. The pastor is meant to deliberately pass on the gospel to other people who can teach it as well. Or rather, who *will be able* to teach it to others. They *will be able* to teach others also. It's a future tense there, because Paul is looking to the future. 'Find some people, Timothy,' says Paul, 'who may not be perfect teachers now. But you can see potential in them. They are faithful in little, so they will be faithful in much. They believe Jesus is the Messiah, and that He rose from the dead to be our everlasting king. They have a passion for that gospel, and are OK with people.' And Paul is careful to add: 'Be strengthened in this endeavour by the grace that is in Christ Jesus. The grace which he gave us in Christ before the very foundation of the world. And in that strength, pass on the baton to those who can carry it forward to the ends of the earth, and to the end of the age.'

---

6. John Richardson and Dub Gannon, *The Deliberate Pastor* (London: Lost Coin, 2016), p. 47.

This is the noble task to which some of us are called. This is why new ministers in the Church of England are given a Bible at their ordination. It's an enormous task. It feels unending. It can feel overwhelming. It *is* beyond us, in our own strength, and it puts us in the firing line. But there's no better way to literally spend your life, than to pour it out like this as an offering to Jesus—who brought life and immortality to light through the gospel.

And what better words to hear, on the great and terrible day of the Lord, when He comes again in the glory of His Father and with the holy angels, than 'Well done, good and *faithful* servant. You have been faithful over little; I will set you over much. Enter into the joy of your master' (Matt. 25:21, 23).

Reaching out to the lost, building something for eternity, and sending others out to join in. What else could you possibly do—for the glory of God and for the good of the world—that's more richly rewarding or more spiritually satisfying or more eternally significant than that?

## Suffering for the gospel

Paul has been writing to Timothy so far about recruitment and gospel succession. Then in verse 3, the apostle tells Timothy to share in *suffering* as a good solider of Christ. This suffering may come as a result of holding fast to the gospel, or indeed, because of his activities in recruiting and training the next generation of leaders too. But this is also just to return to the theme of the letter. In chapter 1 verse 8, Paul told Timothy 'share in suffering for the gospel by the power of God.' It's a major theme throughout this letter. Suffering, persecution, hardship is inevitable if we are to be faithful in ministry.

Yet are we not always tempted to circumvent suffering, and find shortcuts around it? That's the thrust of the next few verses, in these brief illustrations Paul gives us, of the soldier, the athlete, and the farmer. We have to think about these carefully, verse 7 says. But if we do that, the Lord will give us understanding of how they apply.

## The soldier

'No soldier gets entangled in civilian affairs, since his aim is to please the one who enlisted him' (2 Tim. 2:4). A soldier suffers because he has to be focused on war, not on civilian affairs. Soldiers have to think about what pleases their commander, not what pleases them—what serves the war effort, not what makes them cosy. And it's the same with spiritual warfare too, in ministry. We are dedicating ourselves to pleasing God above all. It is not about our creature comforts, and earning a good living as respected professionals and community leaders.

It is not about keeping our heads down and doing the good works that everyone approves of while we fail to speak God's Word and hand it on. Christianity is not just an ethical code, or a way for us to earn a living, but a message of good news about Jesus Christ and His heavenly kingdom.

Paul isn't saying we can't be married or that we can't do tent-making outside of ministry (as he did) or that we have to ignore the world and just read the Bible and pray in our monastic cells. No. Rather, this is about single-mindedly obeying the orders of our captain, Jesus, to preach the Word in season and out of season—regardless of what J. C. Ryle called 'the pressure of incessant official frowns, persecution, ridicule, or unpopularity.'[7] We stand firm and fight on. That's why He gave us a spirit not of cowardice but of power, love and self-discipline (2 Tim. 1:7). Our ultimate reward is His smile of approval, if we persevere.

## The athlete

'An athlete is not crowned unless he competes according to the rules' (verse 5). How many Russian athletes won medals at the Rio Paralympics? None. Because Russia

---

7. See Lee Gatiss (ed.), *Stand Firm and Fight On: J. C. Ryle and the Future for Anglican Evangelicals* (London: Lost Coin, 2016), p. 128.

broke the rules, so none were allowed to compete. Why did the team from Great Britain and Northern Ireland and associated crown dependencies get disqualified from the men's 4x400m relay event in the same Olympics? Because they apparently ran outside the changeover zone, which is against the rules.

Why was Izzat Artykov from Kyrgyzstan stripped of his bronze medal in the weightlifting? Because he tested positive for a banned substance (strychnine) and was disqualified. As anyone who reads Agatha Christie knows, strychnine is of course highly toxic and can kill you in a most unpleasant way. But some people take it as a performance enhancer because it can seem to help the muscles. There must be something of an illustration in here somewhere, about using poisonous doctrine to help boost ecclesiastical performance. But the point is, it's harder to keep the rules than it is to find a way around them to make life easier, give you a boost, or shave a few seconds off your time.

It would be easier not to get up early day after day and hit the gym or the training ground, and use the proper equipment. But did you hear all those who won gold in Rio? 'It was worth all the suffering, just for this moment.' Alex Gregory won gold at Rio for Team GB in the Men's Coxless Four rowing. He wrote a few days later in *Sport Magazine*, 'Four years of pain worth it for six golden minutes.' That is, 'Four years of training seven days a week, 350 days a year. Hundreds of thousands of miles in a boat, millions of hard strokes. Thousands of tonnes of weight lifted, 6,000 calories a day consumed. Hundreds of gallons of sweat lost, and raw, blistered hands every one of those painful days.' And they won. Or as he put it, 'We had triumphed over the struggles and games our minds play on us.'[8]

Athletes in the ancient Olympics had to turn up for ten months before the games, for special training and

---

8. *Sport Magazine*, August 2016.

preparation. And they had to swear on oath that they had finished the training according to the rules.[9] Timothy is to train himself in godliness. And that's not easy or straightforward. But 'while bodily training is of some value, godliness is of value in every way, as it holds promise for the present life and also for the life to come' (1 Tim. 4:8).

Every denomination has rules about the conduct of ministry. Have you looked into what they are for your church? In my own Church of England, ministers have to take vows at their ordination. Not just of allegiance to the King and canonical obedience to the bishop. But even more serious vows, to teach and uphold the doctrine and discipline of the church. Here's how the 1662 *Book of Common Prayer* presents those vows to those who wish to be ordained presbyters:

**The bishop asks:**
WILL you then give your faithful diligence always so to minister the doctrine and sacraments, and the discipline of Christ, as the Lord hath commanded, and as this Church and Realm hath received the same, according to the commandments of God; so that you may teach the people committed to your cure and charge with all diligence to keep and observe the same?

**Answer.** I will so do, by the help of the Lord.

**The bishop:** WILL you be ready, with all faithful diligence, to banish and drive away all erroneous and strange doctrines contrary to God's Word; and to use both public and private monitions and exhortations, as well to the sick as to the whole, within your cures, as need shall require, and occasion shall be given?

---

9. See William D. Mounce, *Pastoral Epistles* (Nashville: Thomas Nelson, 2000), p. 510.

**Answer:** I will, the Lord being my helper.

**The bishop:** WILL you be diligent in prayers, and in reading of the holy Scriptures, and in such studies as help to the knowledge of the same, laying aside the study of the world and the flesh?

**Answer:** I will endeavour myself so to do, the Lord being my helper.

**The bishop:** WILL you be diligent to frame and fashion your own selves, and your families, according to the doctrine of Christ; and to make both yourselves and them, as much as in you lieth, wholesome examples and patterns to the flock of Christ?

**Answer:** I will apply myself thereto, the Lord being my helper.

Whether you're an Anglican like me or not, will you? Will you do these things, God being your helper? The imperishable crown of righteousness (1 Cor. 9:25; 2 Tim. 4:8) awaits those who compete according to these rules.

### The farmer

But third, Paul also compares suffering in ministry to the labour of a hard-working farmer: 'It is the hardworking farmer who ought to have the first share of the crops' (2 Tim. 2:6).

It is not an easy life. It is arduous, strenuous, difficult and taxing. But if you circumvent the suffering, and get lax about the hard work ('well, I can get away with less—who will notice?'), don't bother with the ploughing ('well, nobody else I know spends so long on this sort of thing'), don't prune the vines carefully ('well, I'm not sure that's really my job'), and don't get your hands dirty in some of the unpleasantness ('well, I don't really like that aspect of the job')—then there are consequences.

There are consequences on the last day when the work of each one of us is weighed and assessed, as we all stand before the judgment seat of Christ (2 Cor. 5:10) to give an account for our ministries. Have we reached out to all the lost sheep, or just given a little whistle and left it at that because anything more would be too much effort? Have we built up the church, or just built our own reputations and salaries and nest eggs? Have we sent out workers into the harvest field, or kept all the workers in our own patch because that way we don't have to work so hard?

You may think this is all easy, now. You may be full of naive enthusiasm and youthful vigour for the road ahead. But not everyone can face it. One person I know recently gave up on full-time ministry altogether after three years as a curate and has since retrained in another field. And not all of those that I trained alongside twenty-five years ago have remained in ministry either, for one reason or another. It isn't an easy life.

Paul says, share in the suffering. Because it's worth it. It may well be longer than four years before you see His smile, receive the medal, and eat the fruit of His heavenly kingdom. But if, like Paul, we 'endure everything for the sake of the elect that they also may obtain the salvation that is on Christ Jesus with eternal glory'—then it will all have been worth it.

The saying is faithful and trustworthy (verse 11):
'If we have died with him, we will also live with him.
If we endure, we will also reign with him.'

We stand firm and fight on despite the suffering and death-to-self of Christian ministry, because these things are gloriously true!

But note also what Paul says about his own situation. He is suffering in prison, 'bound with chains as a criminal.' But 'the word of God is not bound' (2 Tim. 2:9). That is an encouragement, in one way. It reminds us that once God's

Word is unleashed, it is utterly unstoppable. That if Timothy entrusts it to reliable and able people back in Ephesus, he can be sure it will continue to thrive even when he's left to stand by Paul in Rome.

But I wonder if it is also a reminder that God doesn't absolutely need us. If we get locked up, or if we turn out to be less than reliable, then God will still achieve His purposes for the elect, and for His glory. Or as verses 12 and 13 put it:

'If we deny him, he also will deny us.

If we are faithless, he remains faithful—for he cannot deny himself.'

Those are words of warning. If we apostatize, fall away, and deny the faith, then we are the ones who lose out. Not God. Not the cause of truth. Those who have abandoned the faith, and sometimes their families as well, in public repudiation of their responsibilities and duties as ministers of the gospel, will hear those dreadful words: 'I never knew you; depart from me, you workers of lawlessness' (Matt. 7:23).

There are some whom I used to look up to as heroes of the faith and outstanding preachers, who have not only given up on ministry but made a shipwreck of their lives, their marriages, and their faith. As Chris Green says, 'Their attitude is probably more indicative of a direction in life than a momentary giving way to pressure, one weakness leading on to further weakness, and an action becoming a cast of mind. It is far better to steel oneself in advance by mulling over this powerful warning.'[10] If it could happen to them, then why not to you? Be awake. Be on guard, against what Alex Gregory called 'the struggles and games our minds play on us.'

Yet maybe we won't deny Him altogether. But it may just be that we will prove to be faithless. Not able to remain steady and firm and endure hardship and suffering and

---

10.   Green, *Finishing the Race*, p. 85.

'incessant official frowns' as resolutely as we hope. Well, in that situation, I think the last line is meant to be an encouragement to us, and to Timothy. If we are faithless, God remains who He was, and is. He is a faithful God. He cannot deny Himself, or the covenant promise by which He has bound Himself to all those who truly repent and believe the gospel.

That's a word to tempted Timothy. Tempted to keep his head down and his mouth closed in a culture and age in which being a full-blooded, Bible-believing Christian was neither easy nor popular. Tempted not to identify with Paul and his teaching or his tactics too closely, because they seem to end in prison. Tempted to go the easy route, and just think of today and not tomorrow, of comfort here and not eternity.

'If we confess our sins, [God] is *faithful* and just to forgive us our sins and to cleanse us from all unrighteousness' (1 John 1:9).

# 4

# Protecting the Flock
## 2 Timothy 2:14-26

Part of the job of a shepherd is not just to feed the sheep, but to protect them. They may need protecting from their own stupidity—sheep are famous for just following each other around, for example, regardless of the wisdom or otherwise of their chosen path. One summer I was up on Hadrian's Wall, and I saw exactly this—a line of sheep just wandered across our path, not going anywhere in particular, and not being led. Who knows whether the barbarian hordes on the other side of the wall came and picked them off, one by one? Jesus saw the crowds He met as sheep without a shepherd, harassed and helpless (Matthew 9:36).

Strangely, sheep also tend to scatter very easily. I saw this one summer too, as I was travelling through the North Pennines, an area of outstanding natural beauty— sheep here, sheep there, sheep all over the place, dotted across the landscape for miles around. Shepherds on quad bikes were trying to gather them together—I guess this is modern shepherding, and much more fun than using an old sheepdog and a stick. But the point was, you need a quad bike to track all the little fluffy monsters down and get them home safely. Jesus told a parable about a lost sheep in open country (Luke 15:1-7).

Sheep may also need protecting from thieves and from wolves. In the context of ministry, that means false teachers, and false teaching. Harassed and helpless sheep, in open country, are in grave danger. As Jesus said, these thieves come in to steal and kill and destroy. They won't be protected by the hired hand, the mercenary, who is just in it for the money, to make a living. They need a good shepherd (John 10:1-18).

2 Timothy 2:14-26 doesn't actually mention sheep at all. But I do think it picks up on these themes from the Gospels, and has some challenging things to say to us in our twenty-first century context. Paul has been instructing his young protégé, Timothy, who is a church leader in Ephesus. He's been telling him how to stand firm and pass on the gospel in a hostile situation, with various gangrenous theologies flying about the place. He's trying to help Timothy to be a good soldier of Christ Jesus, a good shepherd of the flock, while others are only upsetting people's faith.

## Stick to the straight path

The first thing he says is, stick to the straight path. To protect the flock, stick to the straight path, Timothy. Not like Hymenaeus and Philetus, 'who have *swerved* from the truth' (verse 18). Timothy, by contrast, is to stick to the straight path, rightly handling, rightly dividing the Word of truth—literally in verse 15, cutting it straight.

In English we have the word *orthodoxy*, which literally means 'right glory'—giving right glory to God. And so it came to mean right teaching about Him because false teaching doesn't give God His proper glory. And you may have heard the word *orthopraxis*, which means 'right practice,' the kind of Christian life that follows from orthodox belief. Obviously those two things go together. You may also have heard of an orthodontist—a kind of dentist who sets your teeth straight if they're a bit crooked and wonky. Well, the word here translated 'rightly handle' is related to those words. Literally it's ortho-cutting, cutting something straight. Older translations call it 'rightly *dividing* the word of truth.' But it's about more than simply dividing a passage up in our teaching and getting the structure right.

Maybe we should think of it like cutting a piece of cake. You've got to cut the slices properly: not so small it doesn't satisfy, not so big it's indigestible. Or perhaps we're meant to think about cutting stone, or maybe sandwiches. If you've got children you sometimes have to cut the crusts off for them; so sometimes we have to cut things out of our teaching too—false ideas, unnecessary illustrations, too much material. Or maybe, especially in a Roman context, this could refer to cutting a straight road. The Romans were famous for that. And the word in 2 Timothy 2:15 is used in the Greek Old Testament in that very way: Proverbs 3:6 says, 'in all your ways acknowledge God, and he will *make straight* your paths.'

So in 2 Timothy right-cutting means teaching the Bible clearly so that people know the right way to go. It can also have the nuance, then, that our teaching should be clear and understandable. It's about straight talking, not trying to sound clever or dressing things up, cutting it straight so that people know what we're trying to say, and can sort out truth from error.

Whatever other people are doing, stick to the straight road. As for other people, well, even though we might not always see who else is on the Lord's side, God knows. People like Hymenaeus and Philetus will always be popular and successful. But, says verse 19, 'the Lord knows those who are his.'

Actually, this is a quote from the story of Korah's rebellion in Numbers chapter 16. Korah and about 250 well-known prominent leaders in Israel rebelled against Moses and Aaron, God's appointed leaders. It's a great, dramatic story—do have a read through Numbers 16 sometime, and see what I mean! And this quote in 2 Timothy 2:19 comes straight out of that context—God's leaders being challenged by false leaders teaching a subtly different and therefore totally erroneous theology.

What did God do to protect the church? Sorry if this is too much of a spoiler for you, but He set up a very public demonstration to show whose side He was on. The ground literally opened up and swallowed Korah and his co-conspirators who were trying to lead God's people astray. And then fire came from heaven and consumed the 250 prominent laypeople who had sided with Korah as well.

The Lord knows those who are His. And so did everyone else, in Numbers chapter 16.

Now don't you sometimes wish it was that easy in the modern church? If only the ground would open up and swallow all the dodgy vicars in the Church of England! If only a bolt of lightning would fall from heaven and leave just the charred remains of a chasuble where previously there had been heresy. If only the sounding board would fall on the heads of those preaching gangrenous doctrine from ancient pulpits.

Maybe that would be easier, yes. It would certainly make things a bit clearer, and radically cleanse the church. Not that it would permanently cut off the supply of false teachers of course. Because as Hymenaeus and Philetus show us, false teachers are often ex-Bible-believing teachers. They're 'proud of their evangelical roots' maybe. But they've swerved away from them, or 'grown up theologically' as they might (sometimes rather condescendingly) put it. So as long as there are orthodox believers, there'll always be a good supply of people to swerve away.

But the Lord knows those who are His. He won't forsake them. He's given them a spirit of power, of love and of self-control. He'll strengthen them, help them and cause them to stand, upheld by His righteous omnipotent hand.[1] So, says Paul, when it looks as if everyone in the church has abandoned the truth, don't be dismayed. Such rebellions are inevitable. They have a long, long history. But the Lord knows those who are His, even if it's not always so obvious

---

1. From 'How firm a foundation,' attributed to George Keith or R. Keen (1787).

to everybody else. One day it will be. So, trust Him, and keep going on the straight path yourself.

What is that straight path? Well, if false teaching leads to more and more ungodliness, the main effect of teaching the truth will be: 'Let everyone who names the name of the Lord depart from iniquity.' Or as the Master once put it: by their fruits you shall know them (Matt. 7:20).

## Clean up your own act

What is the fruit in our lives? That's where Paul is going next. What he says is, 'Timothy—clean up your own act.' To protect the flock, clean up your own act.

In 2 Timothy 2:20, Paul begins an interesting illustration, about the different kinds of vessels in use in a great house. Some are of gold and silver, some of wood and clay. But what is he illustrating? What are these two kinds of people? I think in the context here, they can only be true and false teachers in the church. Hymenaeus and Philetus in verse 17 are the bad ones. They're wood and clay, dishonourable, and of no use to the master, with their irreverent babble and their ungodliness which only ruins their hearers. The contrast is clear from the words he uses. In verse 14 Paul says not to get into the kind of word battles and quarrels that false teachers love because they 'do no good' or more literally, 'are not *useful*.' Whereas he wants Timothy to be '*useful* to the master' (verse 21).

This poses Timothy a question: which kind of vessel do *I* want to be in God's house, the community of God's people? If he wants to be a vessel for honourable use, set apart as holy, useful to the master and ready for every good work, then what does he have to do? He must *cleanse* himself from what is dishonourable.

Now, does that mean get rid of the false teachers from the church? Should we perhaps be digging holes for them to fall into, *à la* Numbers 16, or something like that? Some people do read it that way. And I think elsewhere Paul is quite clear about church discipline, and especially about ridding the church of false teachers, and those who claim to be Christians but whose lives bring the gospel into disrepute (see 1 Cor. 5, for example, or Titus 3:10-11). Article 26 of the Church of England's *Thirty-nine Articles* is also clear about that. 'It appertaineth to the discipline of the Church,' it says, 'that inquiry be made of evil Ministers, and that they be accused by those that have knowledge of their offences; and finally, being found guilty, by just judgment be deposed.' In any denomination, there ought to be an orderly way of deposing false teachers and those who lead the church into more and more ungodliness.[2]

But I don't think that's what Paul is talking about here in 2 Timothy 2. He's not talking about cleansing the church of false teachers. In the context of verse 19 where he tells us to depart from iniquity, he's talking here about Timothy cleansing himself from false teaching. He wants Timothy to cleanse *himself* (not the church) from what is dishonourable. To clean up his own act, if he wants to be a useful pastor.

That might be a hint that Timothy himself is starting to drift. It's possible, though, as I have said already, that's not because Timothy was a weakling or a timid little thing, but because he was an ordinary Christian experiencing the powerful pull of temptation in a society which cares very little for Jesus and His Word—just like us. Or Paul may just be warning Timothy not to go in that direction. Either way, the point he is making is crystal clear: if you want to be set apart as holy, useful to the Lord in ministry, and ready for every good work it involves some vigorous cleaning.

So let's not get confused by trying to push the illustration of the house and the vessels in ways it wasn't designed to be pushed. It's all about scrubbing ourselves up, washing away the dirt of false teaching, and cleansing our hearts of its poison and pollution. Not many of us will be involved in administering church discipline where we can depose

---

2.    See the excellent booklet on this by Mark Burkill, *Unworthy Ministers: Donatism and Discipline Today* (London: Latimer Trust, 2010).

false teachers. But we can all be involved in cleaning up our own act.

What does that look like in practice? Paul goes on to apply the illustration in the next few verses. He says if we want to be useful to God in ministry, then we need to have *clean legs*. Verse 22 is all about running—or rather, how to cleanse ourselves from what is dishonourable in terms of the way we 'run' our lives: 'So flee youthful passions and pursue righteousness, faith, love, and peace, along with those who call on the Lord from a pure heart.'

I haven't been round many great houses, but every country mansion I've ever visited would, I think, have frowned on visitors running in the corridors. But Paul is keen to encourage running in God's great house. Only, Paul says there are two ways to run. *Flee youthful desires*—run away from them. And *pursue,* or run after some other things in a different direction. If we do this, we'll be cleansing ourselves from what is dishonourable and making ourselves useful to God, ready for every good work.

So what are the two ways to run? First, there's something to run away from. Paul says flee the evil desires of youth. We can make too much of 1 Timothy 4:12 where Timothy is told not to let people despise him because of his 'youth' because that word 'youth,' in the first-century context, can mean anybody under the age of forty. Timothy is not a child. He's a man. But he still has to flee juvenile tendencies and cleanse himself from them if he wants to be useful to God in ministry and serve Him in a pure way. Especially if he is to protect the flock rather than ruining them.

So what are these desires? I thought I would ask someone a bit older, who might have a keener eye for this sort of thing in younger people. So I consulted a big fat commentary on 2 Timothy by two much older men called Jerome Quinn and William Wacker. Quinn is so old, actually, he died about thirty years ago and Wacker had to finish the book for him! So what do they say about the evil desires or evil lusts of youth? Actually they summarize a great deal of what other commentators say about this verse.

> The lusts are not just the sexual excesses to which youths may be particularly inclined but also... impatience, self-assertion, and self-indulgence... not to mention the hunger for novelty; the contempt for routine; the obdurate, implacable intransigence; the agitation verging on violence [and] the lack of prudent measure... which mark the immature (of any chronological age!)

As they rightly conclude, 'The vices just noted are no monopoly of the young.'[3] Yes, it's true that several people seem to think it has something to do with excessive sexual desires. Such desires are strong in young people they say, but need to be resisted by those of whatever age who wish to lead in the church.

It's also a fault of younger people that they can be impatient to get things done. They like to assert themselves and be noticed—to make a name for themselves. Those are certainly temptations that anyone involved in some kind of ministry is likely to face, especially in our fame-obsessed culture where it is easy to build some kind of platform on social media and sound off about anything and everything. And yes, the other things listed by Quinn and Wacker are also important to avoid if we're going to be useful to the Master and ready for any good work. We need to cleanse ourselves from anger towards other people if we're going to minister to them; we'll need to scrub away that contempt for routine and discipline too.

But the observation I want to dwell on a bit further is where they write of the youthful desire of 'hunger for novelty.' Young people always want the latest thing, whether it's the expensive new Nike trainers, the iWatch, the driverless car, the *Back to the Future* hoverboard, the parish newsletter delivery drone, or the Anglican Gold

---

3. Jerome D. Quinn and William C. Wacker, *The First and Second Letters to Timothy* (Grand Rapids: Eerdmans, 2000), pp. 696–7.

package for their Logos Bible Software system. Whatever the latest must-have item is, they must have it.

I think we can get into that mode of thinking with Christian service very easily. So if everybody's reading a certain book, I have to buy a copy. If it's cool to be into Calvin, I'm into Calvin. If it's hip to be into Piper or Packer or Keller, I've got all their books and I've downloaded their talks onto my Apple Watch. Is church planting the next big thing? Then I'm into that. Is it trendy to be a post-millennial preterist credobaptist liturgist? Then I'm there! I'm totally confused, but I'm there!

Now, I'm not saying there's anything wrong with any of those things necessarily. But it's a mark of youth to be into the latest thing, whatever that may be. If it's a good thing, then it can be beneficial. There's nothing wrong with reading a bit of Calvin and listening to Tim Keller. (I also wouldn't mind that Anglican Gold package for my Logos Bible Software system.) It's when these new things become an all-consuming passion that we have to start wondering. Not that rebelling against everything is the answer either of course. That would be equally immature!

When I was at theological college, there was one book (apart from the Bible) which I read once or twice through every year. It's called *A Little Exercise for Young Theologians* by a German professor called Helmut Thielicke (1908–1986). I read it to keep me sane while I was studying. At one point, he writes:

> Do not assume as a matter of course that you believe whatever impresses you theologically and enlightens you intellectually. Otherwise suddenly you are believing no longer in Jesus Christ, but in Luther, or in one of your other theological teachers.[4]

I think that's something we're all prone to do—to believe whatever impresses us theologically and enlightens us

---

4. Helmut Thielicke, *A Little Exercise for Young Theologians* (Carlisle: Paternoster, 1996), p. 31 (chapter 10).

intellectually, without really testing it against the gold standard of God's Word first. Which is why one of the evil desires of youth is the hunger to find a guru. Whether it's an ancient writer or a modern preacher, we Christians are just as prone to this as anyone. It's especially good if one can find a guru who is unappreciated by others, or too difficult for 'lesser minds' to appreciate—just having their huge voluminous works on your shelf will make one seem clever and intellectually refined. Because that's another evil desire of youth—the desire to look good before others, and to seek reputation and glory and a higher place up the pecking order.

Yet Timothy is called to flee all such desires. To scrub them out of his Christian life and his Christian service in order to be useful to his real Master. And instead, he is to run after something else. Cleansing himself, also means pursuing, verse 22, 'righteousness, faith, love, and peace, along with those who call on the Lord from a pure heart.'

The word 'pure' there is related to the word for 'cleanse' back in verse 21. So I think what he's saying is, pursue these excellent virtues of righteousness, faith, love and peace together with anyone else who is trying to cleanse themselves from what is dishonourable. Others are trying to rid themselves of false teaching and false living too. So work together, stick together.

After all, another of the evil desires of youth is to write everybody else off. To say, 'I'm the only truly sound person!' And we can be disapproving or dismissive of others as not quite up to scratch if they're not quite on our wavelength, or not part of our in-crowd. But Paul reminds Timothy here that there are others who have not bowed the knee to the gods of this age or embraced the latest fashion in gangrenous teaching. We need to find such people and pursue godliness and truth alongside them, not hide in a ghetto or a cave like the prophet Elijah and say, 'I'm the only one left—and they're trying to kill me!' What was it God said to Elijah? Something to the effect of 'No Elijah, there are 7000 other people in the church who call on me with a pure heart. Don't be so self-absorbed—go find them!' (see 1 Kings 19:18).

Christians should never be self-assured, self-contained rugged individualists, but seek out other Christians to encourage and be encouraged by as, together, we cleanse ourselves from what is dishonourable.

So, Timothy is to protect the flock by serving his Master purely. Which means he needs to clean his legs, so to speak, so that as he 'runs' his life he flees immature desires and runs after godliness with others.

## Speak with grace

What else does Paul say about cleansing ourselves from what is dishonourable? He goes on to tell Timothy how to speak in God's great house. He tells him to speak with grace. The context is clearly about interacting with others within the church, especially those with whom he might have disagreements. This is how we protect the flock from false teaching.

What Paul says is, if you want to be useful to the Master in ministry and serve Him purely, you will need clean lips, to learn how to speak when you're spoken to. Stick to the straight path; clean up your own act; and speak with grace. Let's look again at verse 23…

> Have nothing to do with foolish, ignorant controversies; you know that they breed quarrels. And the Lord's servant must not be quarrelsome but kind to everyone, able to teach, patiently enduring evil, correcting his opponents with gentleness…

The first thing to note is that in this 'great house' where God's people are, Timothy needs to know his place, if he is to speak with grace. He's not the master of the house. He's the pastor, not the master. Or as verse 24 puts it, he's 'the Lord's Servant' or, more literally, 'the Lord's slave.' Now, that does rather put him in his place! Although, elsewhere in the Bible to be the Lord's Servant is also a great honour. It's a title given to men like Moses, King David, and other prophets and leaders, including the Messiah Himself (Isaiah 49).

Naturally, it's an immense privilege to be the servant of a great and glorious master, even in worldly terms. It carries certain responsibilities. One cannot act any old way in public—your master's reputation would be harmed if you didn't speak or act with the proper dignity and decorum. It would be out of place, for instance, for us to see His Majesty King Charles's servants acting in an uncouth or crude manner in public, dismissing ordinary people as 'plebs,' and that sort of thing.

Well, in the same way, says Paul, the Lord's Servant has a responsibility to speak properly, to cleanse his speech of impurities and inappropriate words and tones. So verse 23 makes perfect sense. Foolish, ignorant controversies should be below the Lord's Servant, especially if they only breed quarrels. The Lord's Servant must not be quarrelsome, an argumentative sort of person, aggressive or confrontational, a theological Rottweiler who pounces on every tiny error or debatable point and grinds his opponents down with his rhetorical teeth. We've all been there I'm sure, in the Bible study or after-church discussion where someone always has to come back to their favourite hobby-horse. I'm sure I've done it myself. But the Lord's Servant must repent of this, and learn when not to get drawn in to such foolish controversies.

Although… sometimes it *is* necessary to debate and discuss things. And in such situations, verse 24 says the Lord's Servant must be courteous—kind and gentle. Yes, he can correct his opponents—there's no sense here of just leaving them to their muddled thinking or outright heresy without even trying to win them round. We must do that—if we care about truth and we care about others, not least those others who are listening in. But we must do it kindly, and gently. 'Patiently putting up with evil,' says

Paul—i.e. we are not to be resentful or bitter, even if our opponents have said or done some despicable things to us in the past, or we think they plan to do so in the future. The Lord's Servant is to let it go, to be like the Master Himself in forgiveness and patience, and gentle perseverance.

When it says he must be 'able to teach,' that's not just about being competent to handle the Bible. This is not a list of qualifications for an elder, such as we might find elsewhere in the Pastoral Epistles (e.g. 1 Tim. 3:1-7 or Titus 1:5-9). The specific context in 2 Timothy is how to interact with false teachers. So what it means here, I think, is that Timothy must ensure that his relationship with people is always sufficiently respectful and dignified that he is *able to teach* them. And, crucially, that they are *able to learn*. Which means cleansing oneself of the tendency to simply assume you know what the other person is saying. Or the inclination to shout at people one disagrees with, to fly off the handle or go into a rage with fiery or abusive rhetoric against them.

Passion and conviction are good things of course— we mustn't be cold and emotionless and just trot out the old doctrinal certainties. But if passion spills over into an inappropriate outburst, or strong conviction turns to arrogant contempt, then the Master's purposes are not served and the hearer... well, they'll never listen again. You'll be vilified and trolled and unfriended and unfollowed. So the Lord's Servant must always ensure that their behaviour merits a hearing, that they are able to teach, and be heard—even if their opponents choose to disagree.

## Be hopeful

So that's how the Lord's Servant is to speak when he's spoken to. He will need clean lips to represent his Master and be useful to Him. But finally, the Lord's Servant must also be hopeful, says verse 25. They must correct their opponents 'with gentleness,' says Paul, always hoping that 'God may perhaps grant them repentance leading to a knowledge of the truth, and they may come to their senses and escape from the snare of the devil, after being captured by him to do his will.'

The Lord's Servants must always be hopeful. Even if it looks like they're getting nowhere with people who oppose their every word, there is still hope. Because God can change people. He can grant them repentance leading to a knowledge of the truth. That, after all, is what He did with us. We too were once ensnared by the devil, captured by him to do his will. We too were fast bound in sin and nature's night, caught in the chains of ignorance, and enslaved to our own passions and desires. But God rescued us if we're Christians. He gave us repentance, turned us around. Our chains fell off, our hearts were free. We were given repentance and a knowledge of the truth which previously we had all rejected.

God is gracious and kind. He was and is to us. Otherwise He would have given up on us a long time ago. Certainly He would have given up on me. I'm a very slow learner. He continues to be merciful as He enables us by His grace to purify ourselves as He commands us here. And He continues to work by grace in others too. He can even turn His greatest enemies into His most ardent followers. The man writing this letter to Timothy should know. I wonder if he smiled as he wrote verse 25 and verse 26?

'Timothy, maybe you're up against some really hateful men and women who despise Christianity and want to throw Christians like you in prison or worse. Maybe they're spitting blood at you now. Maybe it feels like you're banging your head against a brick wall as you talk to them about Jesus and the gospel.

'But God can change them, you know. He can grant them repentance, and turn them around. Look at me, my beloved child, look at me. And remember what God did in my life one bright day on the road to Damascus.

'I don't know who your opponents will be, Timothy, after I'm dead and buried and you're on your own with all these wayward sheep and false teachers in the church. Maybe they will deny the resurrection, downplay God's judgment on sin, pervert the grace of God into a licence for immorality, and exchange the glorious Father for a goddess fashioned in their own likeness. But don't give up on them. Be courteous and kind and point them to Jesus, and who knows? Who knows?

'Cleanse yourself from the dishonourable thought that there's no point with these people anymore. If God is God and they're still alive, there's hope.'

What a great message for us as Christians. The good news of Jesus as we have received it seems to have been rejected by our society and even by large parts of the church. But don't panic, says Paul. Don't give up. There is still hope: God may grant repentance. God is a God of surprises, a God who delights to turn things around. He's an expert in resurrections and transformations.

So as we wait for Him to act, let's serve the Master purely, and cleanse ourselves of everything that spoils our witness to His truth. Let's protect the flock entrusted to our care and stick to the straight path. Clean up our own act, speak with grace and always pray with hope.

# 5

# Keep Calm and Carry On

## *2 Timothy 3*

Jesus said, 'every scribe who has been trained for the kingdom of heaven is like a master of a house, who brings out of his treasure what is new and what is old' (Matt. 13:52). My friend John Richardson was just such a teacher, and in the last few years of his ministry he was fond of quoting an old 1945 Church of England report called *Towards the Conversion of England.* This recognized the need for change in the Church itself. It said:

> The really daunting feature of modern evangelism… is not the masses of the population to be converted, but that most of the worshipping community are only half-converted. The aim of evangelism must be to appeal to all, within as well as without the Church, for that decision for Christ which shall make the state of salvation we call conversion the usual experience of the normal Christian.

The Church of England—it said—is, however:

> ill-equipped for its unparalleled task and opportunity. The laity complain of a lack of creative leadership among all ranks of the clergy. The spiritual resources of the community are at a low ebb. Above all, the Church has become confused and uncertain in the proclamation of its message, and its life has ceased to reflect clearly the truth of the Gospel (paragraph 33).

If I am judging the times rightly, I think this need is even more pressing in our day than it evidently was in 1945—and not just for the Church of England but for every denomination. That's why the vision of the Junior Anglican Evangelical Conference (JAEC) which John Richardson founded was the rededication of the Church of England to the proclamation of the gospel, that all may be reached in every parish. We want to be part of a movement of reformation and renewal which sees that as the goal. But this is not going to be quick or easy.

The JAEC conferences and our ongoing discussions in a Facebook network group, recognize the need to deepen our understanding of our Anglican heritage and to engage critically but positively with it as we work across 'party lines' within evangelicalism. We want to identify, encourage and equip a future generation of evangelical denominational leaders, to proclaim afresh in our generation that faith revealed in the Holy Scriptures to which the historic formularies of the Church of England bear witness. There are similar movements in other denominations.

In JAEC, we want to be loyal to this inheritance of faith as our inspiration and guidance under God in bringing the grace and truth of Christ to this generation and making Him known to those in our care (as all Church of England ministers are meant to, according to canon law).[1] As John Richardson said at the 2011 Conference,

> The Church of England is still viable. It still has thousands of ministers and hundreds of thousands of members. Its parishes cover the entire nation and in some areas, particularly in the countryside, it is the only remaining visible Christian presence. It is worth fighting for!
>
> Evangelicals ought to be at the forefront of evangelism. It is only a ministry which seeks conversions that deserves the label 'evangelical.' But they ought also to be aiming at nothing less than making the Church of England itself

---

1. See Canon C15.

'evangelical.' If we are content to thrive in our small corner whilst the national church remains indifferent to the task of evangelism, we truly care neither for our own beliefs nor for the people of our nation as a whole.

Church Society, of which I am the Director, exists to resource those who share this evangelical vision, that we may be confident in the gospel, as well as equipped and empowered to share it—in and through the Church of England. We pray that it may lead and enable others, as the Anglican Ordinal puts it, 'to seek for Christ's sheep... that they may be saved through Christ for ever.' But if that is to happen, whether in the Church of England or outside it, we will need a new reformation. We are not romantic antiquarians in a re-enactment society, pining for the past and being grumpy about the present because it fails to live up to our dreams. Emphatically, no. We must be forward looking, energetic reformers, eager to serve God in our generation, and therefore to engage at every level of the church, that it might become a more effective instrument in the Holy Spirit's hands for the Holy Spirit's work. That's what every denomination needs.

And yet as we go about these tasks, as Paul says in our reading, we live in terrible times. 'But understand this, that in the last days there will come times of difficulty' (2 Tim. 3:1). So if we are to accomplish the goal of reforming and renewing our churches in biblical faith today, we must properly judge the times in which we live, avoid charlatans in the church, endure suffering in godly imitation, and continue using the Bible in every ministry.[2]

## Judge the times in which we live

There is a website online which tracks forty-five signs of the end times, called 'The Rapture Index.' It claims to provide a 'prophetic speedometer of end-time activity' so that users

---

2.  The four points of this chapter mirror the main points of 2 Timothy 3, but, yes, their initial letters also spell out JAEC. What can one do, when this just coincidentally happens?!

can be aware of how close we are getting to the climactic moment. In October 2016, with hurricanes and floods and economic turbulence and ongoing war in Syria, it hit a record high rating of 189, which indicates a fasten your seat-belts moment as we speed towards the pre-tribulation rapture (apparently). I wonder what the index is today, as you read this?

The Rapture Index tracks various things Jesus mentions in the Gospels, although I am not convinced this is the best way for us to apply what He says. But many of these indicators certainly are features of our world today: wars, insurrections, earthquakes, famines, plagues, and a multitude of Messiahs full of empty promises and lies. And worse than that, the persecution of believers (see Luke 21:5-19).

With the uncertainties of the post-Brexit world, the polarization of politics on both sides of the Atlantic, a persistent terrorist threat, and the renewed spectre of potential confrontations between nuclear powers... not to mention the alarming decline in church attendances recently reported by the press, the shocking nature of victimization experienced by Christians in many parts of the world, and the appalling spectacle of sexual politics in the church—it is tempting to say that we live in peculiarly terrible times.

Some people have likened our current situation to the days just prior to the evangelical revival of the eighteenth century. Church attendances had fallen. The clergy were worldly or asleep. So they hope and pray for another great awakening to revitalize the church of God and expand her boundaries, as happened in those heady days of George Whitefield and John Wesley.

Others see a better comparison with the church in the early years of the sixteenth century, before Martin Luther came along and the gospel split Western Christendom in two. Are we not seeing another division of this magnitude today, as some rally to the truth and others reject it? Should we not pray for such clarity to grow?

Many who also take into account the increasingly anti-Christian bias of the Western world, see our situation as more akin to that of the churches of Northern Africa before the sweeping victories of Islam wiped them out in the seventh and eighth centuries. That's a more depressing thought, isn't it? But is that not what we are seeing—the demise of Christianity in the West, in the face of secularism and resurgent Islam? Is it not now inevitable?

Sometimes there are patterns in history which do repeat themselves, simply because God in His holiness and truth has not changed, and humanity in all its sinfulness has consistently remained the same. So are there lessons for us to learn in the Bible, about how to respond and behave when we find ourselves in difficult times?

In what was possibly one of his last letters, the Apostle Paul wrote to Timothy about this very issue. 'There will come times of difficulty,' he said. And he wanted to equip his junior colleague to distinguish faithful ministry from the corrupt self-serving of others which would not advance the cause of Christ.

He speaks in the future tense about 'the last days.' What does he mean? He could be talking about what will happen in the very last days before Jesus comes again to wrap things up and make all things new. But in verse 5, after outlining what people will be like in those last days, he speaks to Timothy in the present tense. And in verse 6 he goes on to indicate that the people he is talking about are operating right now in Timothy's present.

So perhaps 'the last days' are not just those near the very end of time, but an extended period, including apostolic times down to the end—from the ascension to the second coming? Another intriguing possibility suggested by the great seventeenth-century scholar, John Owen, is that Paul is referring to the last days of the Jewish church-state, so to speak. The last days before the Temple was destroyed in accordance with Jesus' prophecy, and that old dispensation was completely gone forever. Timothy was living in those times, and needed to be aware of what they would be like. That wouldn't make this all irrelevant for us of course (Owen still manages to apply this chapter to ministry in the post-A.D. 70 world). But it is an intriguing suggestion.[3]

Paul speaks about false teachers who have 'swerved from the truth,' and about the effects of their gangrenous teaching. He goes on to talk about those who worm their way into households to scratch itching ears with their attractive and desire-affirming messages, because 'the time is coming when people will not endure sound teaching.' This pattern seems to me to have been the universal experience of the church throughout the last 2000 years, or more, not something restricted to the first century. Though if there is an intensification of such corruption immediately before the return of the Lord, that would not be a surprise.

If Paul thought Timothy needed to be on guard here, can we afford to ignore his warnings? We are living in difficult times. We need to understand that, so it doesn't take us by surprise. God knew it would be like this and He warned us. In 1 Timothy 4 Paul says 'the Spirit expressly says that in later times some will depart from the faith.' So if the Spirit has expressly spoken, it is foolish of us to naively think it will be different for us. So judge the times in which we live rightly. It will never be plain sailing.

### Avoid charlatans in the church

Secondly, what does Paul say we should do in these times? My second point is that if we are to reform and renew the church in these last days, for the glory of God and the good of His world, we must avoid charlatans in the church.

Who is he warning against? 2 Timothy 3 begins with what sounds like a general condemnation of 'people' in the

---

3.  W. H. Goold (ed.), *The Works of John Owen* (Edinburgh: Johnstone and Hunter, 1854), 20:11 (commenting on Heb 1:2); citing 1 Timothy 4:1; 2 Peter 3:3; 1 John 2:18; Jude 18. cf. *Works*, 9:322; 17:542-43.

last days. People will be lovers of self, lovers of money, lovers of pleasure rather than lovers of God. And then, verse 5, he says 'Avoid such people.'

I thought at first this was a list of qualities describing secular and worldly people. The sins of unbelievers with misdirected loves. It's easy to see our world in verses 2-5. People fitting these descriptions appear on our TVs every night on the news. Arrogant, abusive, heartless, slanderous, brutal—just scroll through social media for a bit or read the newspapers. That's the way of the world this side of the Fall. It's because we're all like this, that Christ had to die.

But I'm not so sure Paul is critiquing the world here, and telling us to avoid it. I think he is actually talking with prophetic insight about the heretics Timothy was dealing with in Ephesus. That is, people who claimed to be true spiritual leaders, but were not. Paul wrote to the Corinthians about these people too, remember? He says in 1 Corinthians 5:9-13:

> I wrote to you in my letter *not to associate* with sexually immoral people— not at all meaning the sexually immoral of this world, or the greedy and swindlers, or idolaters, since then you would need to go out of the world. But now I am writing to you *not to associate* with anyone who bears the name of brother if he is guilty of sexual immorality or greed, or is an idolater, reviler, drunkard, or swindler— not even to eat with such a one. For what have I to do with judging outsiders? Is it not those inside the church whom you are to judge? God judges those outside. 'Purge the evil person from among you.'

So the Corinthians can't avoid immoral people in the world without going out of the world—i.e. when Paul told them to 'avoid such people' he didn't mean don't ever talk to non-Christians. What he meant was, don't associate with people who live worldly lives but who claim at the same time to be Christians. Those are the ones to avoid, because they are inauthentic pretenders, fraudsters, who give a false impression about the gospel of repentance and faith, and fail to inculcate the holiness of Christ.

Our associations matter. We've already seen that in this letter, because Paul mentions those who have declined to associate themselves with him in his hour of need, and praised those who have chosen to stand by him. The whole letter is a call to loyalty. And he says to Timothy that he needs to avoid entangling associations with certain people.

It quickly becomes apparent that he has his eye especially on certain spiritual leaders, who creep insidiously into the homes of the vulnerable. These charlatans seek to capture their unguarded prey for never-ending programmes of false teaching and pastorally cruel deception. Their agenda is centred on people's longings—that is, those who are 'burdened with sins and led astray by various passions' (2 Tim. 3:6) and accumulate teachers to suit those desires (chapter 4:3). They wander away from the truth into mythical superstition and potted this-worldly wisdom which allows them to satisfy their cravings.

Counterfeit religion tries to help people fulfil their desires, and avoid any tensions or suffering in the here and now. Yet it gives its devotees chewing gum for food, so that they are always learning (and probably being charged handsomely to do so) but never able to swallow a knowledge of the truth. We were designed, someone once taught me, to open our minds for the same reason that we open our mouths— to close them again on something solid. But keeping the conversation going, always stimulating but never satisfying, is the hallmark of those who intrude themselves like cuckoos into the household of God. Avoid such charlatans in the church, Timothy, says Paul. They oppose the truth, have corrupted minds, and are disqualified regarding the faith.

This could be tricky because, in the previous chapter, Paul had a more 'redemptive approach' (as Philip Towner puts it).[4] Timothy was told in chapter 2 to not be quarrelsome, but correct his opponents with gentleness, teaching and praying for them. But I think the people in view here in chapter 3 are the more hardened ringleaders. The hardcore 'leading spokespeople' who can no longer be reached, who have set themselves implacably to oppose true ministry and true ministers, and resolutely act in ways indistinguishable from the worldliness in verses 2-5. You may be wondering how to tell the difference between the charlatans we avoid and the opponents we correct with gentleness. It may be a wisdom call in some cases. But I think in general it becomes clearer and clearer. There is a stubbornness, an incorrigibility, an unteachableness about the former.

Now how do you think we apply this? What do you think? I think this means we mustn't be naive. While those of us who are in it may want to have a positive approach to the Church of England today, for example, to engage wherever we can and be properly optimistic in accordance with the gospel, there are going to be people we have to avoid. As I say in the book *Be Faithful*:

> There may be times when, if we are to be faithful to the Lord Jesus, we will be forced to *defend* the truth of God's word in public, even when it is uncomfortably counter-cultural. We will need to *disassociate* ourselves from false teaching and those who propagate it, however painful that may be—particularly today from those who would deceive us on issues of sexual conduct by trying to recalibrate our morality (Ephesians 5:3-7). We must *disobey* orders which contradict Christ's or bless what God has not. We must enforce godly *discipline*, driving out those who are recalcitrantly immoral and leading others astray (1 Corinthians 5:9-13). We must peacefully *disrupt* and financially degrade the capabilities of those who scandalise the church and seek to undermine its foundations from within. And we must in every way *deny* the deadly doctrine underpinning such attempts

---

4.  Philip Towner, *The Letters to Timothy and Titus* (Cambridge: Eerdmans, 2006), p. 561.

to turn the grace of God into a license for immorality (Jude 4).[5]

Avoid charlatans in the church. But flee youthful passions and pursue righteousness, faith, love and peace along with those who call on the Lord from a pure heart—whether they agree with you in every detail or not.

But notice, too, the rather hopeful note at the end of this section, in verse 9. In Paul's day, Jannes and Jambres were the names by which the Egyptian magicians who opposed Moses during the Exodus, were known. The charlatans are just like them, says Paul, in their opposition to you. And just like Jannes and Jambres, they will not succeed in the end. Their folly will be plain to all.

Really Paul?

That must have been hard to believe at times.

For Athanasius, for example, in the fourth century, when he endured exile after exile and often seemed to be defeated by the heretical Arians ruling the church of his day. Yet the Nicene Creed is the unquestioned standard of orthodoxy all over the world today.

It must have been hard for Luther too, to believe verse 9— when the establishment railed against him and threatened him and hauled him up in front of the imposing majesty of the Emperor and his court. But I think he would giggle contentedly if he could see Reformation-inspired churches 500 years later.

It must have been hard for Thomas Cranmer to read verse 9 as well—when his monarch and his monasteries and his clergy kept getting in the way of his efforts to reform the Church of England, and in the end he was imprisoned and executed, never seeing the turnaround to come some years later.

We don't always receive what is promised, in this life. Sometimes vindication awaits another century, or a future

---

5.   Lee Gatiss, Mike Ovey, and Mark Pickles, *Be Faithful: Remaining Steadfast in the Church of England Today* (London: Lost Coin, 2017), p. 71.

judgment. But it will come. The folly of charlatans *will* be exposed: maybe not today, maybe not tomorrow; but one day their infamy will be obvious for eternity.

So avoid them. With these people, make the distinctions of eternity plain in the present, as if these were the very last days.

## Endure suffering in godly imitation

And then in verse 10, Paul says, 'Because these false teachers have infiltrated the church; because they have convinced many, and seem to be making progress; because their message is more palatable to the powers that be... you should probably give up now. It's a lost cause, so walk away, and try something different. Shake the dust off your feet, and go somewhere else where they'll really appreciate your ministry instead.'

No, he doesn't say that, does he?

Timothy must fulfil his ministry—which will most certainly involve the endurance of suffering, until the arrival of God's heavenly kingdom. In a series of contrasts in the second half of the chapter, Paul urges his junior colleague to stand out from this sickening ecclesiastical culture he has described.

First, he is to stand out by enduring suffering in godly imitation. This means Timothy is to remember that a godly life is not one free from pain—it involves suffering in this world as we long for the next: the suffering of persecution, the agony of putting to death our disordered and disorderly desires, and the nauseating necessity of confronting and refuting the decadence of heresy.

But Paul has been calling Timothy to do that throughout this letter. In chapter 1 he set the tone by saying in verse 8, 'share in suffering for the gospel by the power of God.' Then in chapter 2 he talked about enduring suffering for the sake of the elect, and how, if we endure, we will also reign with Christ.

Now, he reminds Timothy of his own example again, calling him implicitly to follow in it. He says in verses 10-13:

> You, however, have followed my teaching, my conduct, my aim in life, my faith, my patience, my love, my steadfastness, my persecutions and sufferings that happened to me at Antioch, at Iconium, and at Lystra—which persecutions I endured; yet from them all the Lord rescued me. Indeed, all who desire to live a godly life in Christ Jesus will be persecuted, while evil people and impostors will go on from bad to worse, deceiving and being deceived.

Timothy is Paul's beloved child in the faith, and has been his apprentice in ministry for many years. He knows how Paul has done things, and what he has had to endure. He's followed it closely. Paul speaks about what happened to him in Antioch, Iconium, and Lystra, bringing to mind particular episodes for Timothy to recall.

At Iconium (we're told in Acts 14), Paul was opposed by a strong Jewish faction, who stirred up the city, poisoned people's minds against the gospel, and got a coalition of Jews and Gentiles together to try and stone him. Interesting pattern: religious opponents joining hands with unbelievers to attack those who speak the truth.

Then at Lystra, some Jews came from Antioch and Iconium to again persuade the crowds against Paul, and they succeeded in having him stoned and dragged out of the city and left for dead. He rose up and eventually left for Derbe.

Then rather extraordinarily, Paul and Barnabas, *went back* to Lystra, and to Iconium, and to Antioch 'strengthening the souls of the disciples, encouraging them to continue in the faith, and saying that through many tribulations we must enter the kingdom of God' (Acts 14:22).

He didn't give up. He was a Chumbawamba Christian. He got knocked down, but he literally got up again.[6] And

---

6.  Please forgive a reference to the anarchist punk band Chumbawamba, and an allusion here to a line from their hit 'Tubthumping' (1997)!

then he bravely went back to those same places to encourage the believers there to stand firm. Because everyone who wants to live a godly life in Christ Jesus *will* be persecuted. It happened to Paul and Barnabas. It happened to others in the New Testament. It even happened to the Lord of Glory Himself.

This is a message for the snowflake generation, isn't it? There are no 'safe spaces' for Christians anymore, if there ever were. People will not happily embrace the gospel on every street corner, or even allow it a dignified hearing in some places. We will not triumph over darkness with undisturbed tranquility and smoothness. And we will not go floating up to heaven on flowery beds of ease.

It's going to be hard. These are difficult times. There will be friction. And there might be literal sticks and stones to break your bones, as well as harsh words said against you, if you try to speak clearly and openly about Christ. But only if you try to live a godly life in Christ Jesus, of course. If you water down the gospel you preach so that it doesn't contain a message of repentance anymore, then you might get away more easily. If your gospel affirms people where they're at and doesn't call them to change, it might be better. If you teach love of self, love of money, love of pleasure rather than sorrow for sin, sackcloth and sanctification, then you'll be fine. But all who desire to live a godly life in Christ Jesus, and teach others the same—Will. Be. Persecuted.

So be prepared to share in suffering as a good soldier of Christ Jesus. Endure it, in imitation of our Lord Himself, of His apostles and prophets, and of our martyred forebears. We bear the torch that flaming fell from the hands of those, who gave their lives proclaiming that Jesus died and rose.[7]

## Continue using the Bible in every ministry

Finally, in another contrast with the charlatans, Paul also tells Timothy not to give up on his teaching ministry.

---

7. See 'Facing a task unfinished' by Frank Houghton (1894–1972).

Standing firm in the faith involves standing firm in the inspired and sufficient Scriptures, the sword of the Spirit which is the Word of God. Or as Paul says in verses 13-17:

> evil people and impostors will go on from bad to worse, deceiving and being deceived. But as for you, *continue* in what you have learned and have firmly believed... All Scripture is breathed out by God and profitable for teaching, for reproof, for correction, and for training in righteousness, that the man of God may be complete, equipped for every good work.

So my final point is: continue using the Bible in every ministry. This, I imagine, is in contrast to what Paul calls in 1 Timothy 6:20 'the irreverent babble and contradictions of what is falsely called "knowledge"' (see also 2 Tim. 2:16). It is in contrast to the message being preached by the charlatans—who may glance at the Bible where it is profitable to do so, and fling the odd verse around when it's useful to their cause; but has imposed a worldly agenda on the church, replacing the sword that makes the wounded whole with one that never heals because it never cuts.

The faith of the Scriptures teaches us to live differently to those described at the start of this chapter. Even though Timothy has known this since childhood, Paul realizes that the temptation to drift into a piety which acknowledges the Bible in some way but does not bow meekly to its supreme God-breathed authority, is a very real danger. Even Timothy, it would seem, was not invulnerable to the temptation to slip anchor and wander away from his moorings in the Scriptures. He was not to let the world set the tempo for his discipleship; nor must the flesh dictate the programme for his ministry. We must continue using the Bible in every ministry, because it alone is profitable—for teaching, correcting and training people in true righteousness. Anything else will leave us at a loss.

When we try to find alternative sources to teach people righteousness, we inevitably end up dancing to a tune that is alien to the harmonies of heaven. What the world regards as righteous and good and politically correct may often be at odds with what God says in His Word.

The Bible is not only supreme as the voice of our Master Himself, but also utterly sufficient. It was sufficient for Timothy's salvation, says the apostle: it made him wise for salvation in Christ. And it is sufficient also for his ministry in terrible times. He doesn't require the tricks of the false teaching trade to win a hearing or wean people onto healthier doctrine. He is not to 'appreciate his Scriptural heritage and upbringing' but then veer off in a new direction. Continue, says Paul, with that life-giving, unerring Word, even when it doesn't seem to be trendy or palatable.

His opponents may tell him that he needs to be more relevant to modern people. But if Jesus is coming again to judge the living and the dead, what could possibly be more relevant to every single one of us, than the biblical gospel of repentance and faith in Him?

In a world that loves pleasure rather than God, and a church that has the form of godliness but rarely its reality, that is the message we need to hear. So Timothy is not to put it to one side, thinking something else might work better. Pragmatism can never trump God's Word. Constant, consistent biblical teaching is the only thing that makes us, as ministers, competent and equipped for every good work.

## An agenda for reform and renewal

So what are we to do if we want to reform and renew the church in biblical faith today? Paul says:

1. Judge the times in which we live
2. Avoid charlatans in the church
3. Endure suffering in godly imitation
4. Continue using the Bible in every ministry

'Evildoers and impostors will go from bad to worse,' says Paul. We shouldn't be surprised when false religion spreads its noxious fumes in the wake of any authentic work of God. But we are to keep our heads, not buying into the idea that Christianity is inevitably doomed in the sulphuric atmosphere of our contemporary culture. We must persevere in the work of the gospel, whether we see the fruit of our faithfulness immediately or not. For we know in the end that there is nothing more certain than the safety and joy of God's heavenly kingdom, beyond the temporary turmoils of our time.

Those who follow the Apostle Paul's teaching and practice these days are sometimes told they are 'on the wrong side of history.' But ultimately there is no wrong side of history, because history is a conveyer belt and we're all on it, moving inexorably forward to the judgment seat of Christ. The question is not which side of history are you on, but which side of Christ will you be on, on that day.

A few years after Paul wrote to Timothy, the Lord Jesus Himself wrote to Timothy's church.[8] He had some things to say about the enthusiasm of their love for Him. But He noted their intolerance and their discernment regarding false apostles, *because* (I think) they paid attention to 2 Timothy 3. The ascended Christ said to the church in Ephesus:

> I know your works, your toil and your patient endurance, and how you cannot bear with those who are evil, but have tested those who call themselves apostles and are not, and found them to be false. I know you are enduring patiently and bearing up for my name's sake, and you have not grown weary. (Rev. 2:2-3)

Will that be us? On judgment day will He call us together during that heavenly conference and praise us for avoiding the charlatans who operated outrageously under the aegis

---

8.   He may even have been writing to Timothy himself. The letter in Revelation 2 is written to 'the angel of the church at Ephesus,' which most probably refers to the senior elder there, and that may possibly have still been Timothy.

of His church? Will He tell us how He noticed our patient endurance for His name's sake, and our unflagging zeal for the truth which leads to godliness? Will He rejoice that we used His unerring Word in the way that He intended us to—to teach and guide His elect, that they may obtain salvation with eternal glory?

# 6

# Fulfil Your Ministry

## *2 Timothy 4*

I think the big message of what Paul is saying to Timothy here is this: Preach the Word, like I have, amidst the disappointments and dangers, because Jesus is coming again.

So to begin with, the apostle issues a solemn charge to his junior protégé: preach the Word! He expands a little what that might look like. And then he talks about himself and how he has proclaimed the message of the gospel, despite opposition and disappointments from various people. He is an example of what he is urging Timothy to do.

Throughout the chapter, pervading the whole, is the sense that everything is coloured by the second coming of Christ. So the charge to preach is 'in view of his appearing and his kingdom.' Paul, who may be about to face the final curtain in Rome, is convinced that there is a day of judgment and reward to come. And that the Lord will bring him safely to His heavenly kingdom.

So, preach the Word, like I have, amidst the disappointments and dangers, because Jesus is coming again. We could just work our way through the chapter like this. However, if you will allow me, we'll look at it slightly more thematically, under four headings: the context of ministry; the content of ministry; the conduct of ministry; and the consolation of ministry.

## The context of ministry

So first, what is the context of ministry, according to Paul? What sort of world do we live in?

We live the wrong side of Jesus' second coming, where disappointments and difficulties must be expected. His kingdom has not yet come, in the way we pray for it to come in the Lord's Prayer. So although everything that happens in this vale of tears is part of God's plan, this world is not as it should be.

How is that manifested? We see throughout the chapter that life is not easy for those who follow Jesus. It seems like Paul is on his way out, about to die, 'poured out as a drink offering' having fought the good fight and finished the race. Death is an intruder, who will have no place in Christ's heavenly kingdom.

Paul is also in prison, on trial because of his open preaching of the gospel. Which is obviously not right. But the biggest cause of turbulence in all this is people. Because ministry is always about individuals, even if you're an apostle. That's why Paul mentions so many individuals by name in this letter: Timothy's mother and grandmother, Phygelus and Hermogenes, Onesiphorus, Hymenaeus and Philetus, and all those named in this chapter too.

And just as *people* are the greatest source of encouragement in gospel ministry... so also are they the greatest source of trouble and strife. Timothy and Luke, who stayed with Paul, and Mark who was so useful to him in ministry, and Priscilla and Aquila, and the others: they are a source of encouragement. But Paul faces frustrating opposition from others. Some strongly oppose his message (2 Tim. 4:15). Alexander the coppersmith has done him a great deal of harm. That's not how the specially appointed ambassador of the Lord Jesus Christ is meant to be treated. Was this Alexander the same Alexander who opposed Peter and John in Acts 4? Or the Alexander who tried to speak against Paul in Ephesus, in Acts 19? Or the Ephesian Alexander who blasphemed and rejected a good conscience and shipwrecked his faith, whom Paul mentions as having been 'handed over to Satan' in 1 Timothy 1? Whether he's one of them, or another Alexander, he was a pain in the neck and strongly opposed the gospel. We need to watch out for such people, and be aware that they exist.

Certain people have also deserted Paul, he says. He's not just lonely because some of his friends and co-workers have been *sent* elsewhere, or are ministering elsewhere, or are ill (like Tychicus, Mark and Trophimus). No. Paul says, 'Demas, in love with this present world has deserted me and gone to Thessalonica.' Demas is mentioned as one of Paul's co-workers in Colossians 4. But he has not longed for Christ's appearing and loved that, ordering everything he does by the light of that day. He's in love with 'this present world' and its enjoyments and allurements and benefits and methods. So he would not stand by Paul. That's why the apostle says to Timothy, 'Do your best to come to me soon, *unlike* Demas, who won't because he cares more about his comfort and reputation and advancement in this life.' Coming to Paul, being associated with him, shows you're not interested in this present world so much as in the next.

This is what ministry is like: it can be messy and exasperating and disheartening because it's all about dealing with fallen people. We must be prepared for that. This world is not as it should be, and neither is the church.

Evangelicals are especially prone perhaps to thinking about ministry in terms of reading books and writing sermons. The only struggle there is working out what we will say, what is this passage about, how do I teach this subject, will I get it all done in time etc. But ministry is about teaching the Bible *to people*. Ah, now there's the rub!

Paul warns us that not everyone will like what we say. So, he says, 'the time will come when people will not put up with sound doctrine. Instead, to suit their own desires, they will gather around them a great number of teachers to say what their itching ears want to hear. They will turn

their ears away from the truth and turn aside to myths.'
As Douglas Milne says of these people in his commentary
on 2 Timothy, 'Instead of beginning with God's Word and
submitting themselves humbly to its light and truth to
straighten out their thinking and the way they live, they
reverse the process by starting with their own corrupt
passions and unexamined prejudices against the truth, then
seek out teachers to confirm them in their errors and sins.'[1]
And if you're not one of those teachers... they won't listen
to you, however good your sermons and Bible studies are.

We'll think more about this in a moment. But this,
then, is the context of ministry. It's going to be hard. There
will be mental toil, yes. But more than that, there will be
opposition, personal disappointments, and sometimes an
agonising sense that some people just aren't listening.

I think of those I've studied the Bible with and prayed
for over the years. Some have persevered. Others have
faltered, given up ministry because of moral failings; or
because they realized they could earn more a different
way; or because they lost confidence in gospel ministry as
the way to change the world; or because it was always just
about self-fulfilment, and they've now discovered a more
fulfilling profession. We can all see the temptations.

Calvin concludes that, 'having been told that men will
thus despise and even reject the word of God, we ought
not to stand amazed as if it were a new spectacle.'[2] And
yet I've often heard, and seen people say on social media,
something like, 'I didn't expect it to be like this when I was
ordained! Things were different then. This is radically new.'
Well, what does Paul say? Should we be aghast that things
have got so bad in the church? And what are we to do? If
that's the *context* of ministry, what, secondly, is the *content*
of ministry? What should we be doing?

---

1.    Douglas J. W. Milne, *1 Timothy, 2 Timothy, Titus* (Fearn: Christian Focus
Publications, 1996), p. 175.

2.    Calvin, *Commentaries on the Epistles to Timothy, Titus, and Philemon*, p. 255.

## The content of ministry

Paul says, preach the Word. It sounds mundane, but it's anything but. Listen to the big deal blockbuster music playing in the background as he introduces his major strategy for saving the world: 'In the presence of God and of Christ Jesus, who will judge the living and the dead, and in view of his appearing and his kingdom, I give you this charge...'

It's got to be something big and important after this kind of introduction, hasn't it? God is watching, God is here. Jesus is standing next to you. The Jesus who will one day weigh your life in the balance and judge the thoughts and intentions of all, whether alive or dead, and decide your eternal fate, in heaven or in hell. He is coming back, to the world which crucified and rejected Him, coming back as king to rule it.

So as you think about His kingdom, and what's going to happen on that great and terrible day of the Lord... what should you do?

'Preach the word.'

That's right. It's that simple. Open your Bible.

In 2 Timothy 3, Paul told Timothy that in the terrible times of the last days, he was to avoid charlatans in the church, endure suffering, and continue in the kind of Bible ministry that he had known since his infancy. The Word of God is utterly sufficient to save us in Christ and train us in righteousness. It makes us competent and equipped. So our strategy as ministers of the gospel, in a context where people desert and oppose the truth, is remember that Christ is returning, so preach His Word.

There are lots of suggestions these days of strategies for renewal and reform of the church. Someone once told me that getting people to sing psalms more often was *the* way to revolutionize things. Another person told me that the key to everything is good liturgy. I'm sure they have their place. Some are convinced that what we need is more celebrity

Christians, being a good example in the public sphere. Others think we also need great apologists to appear on TV, or to have our case put forcefully and eloquently in *The Guardian* or *The Telegraph* or on the *Victoria Derbyshire* programme and *Newsnight*. That will do it. That's what we really need in this hour, and without such a national presence we are failing.

Some are persuaded that we really need pure platforms, some new 'safe spaces' where we can propagate our views without having to deal with internal opposition or worrying about people who disagree with us. If only we could start again, strike out on our own, and with a clean slate and a pristine pulpit do things our way... *then* we'd really make progress.

Or perhaps what we need are more big 'resource churches,' as thriving hubs in town centres, with good music and good coffee and beautiful people. Others think that cultural engagement and social action will do the business. Faithful presence in an alien culture will slowly transform things for the better, as people see that we're not so bad really and the gospel is a good and positive influence.

Many, of course, believe that we have to update the message, to make it more commercially viable in today's marketplace of ideas, where sexual freedom, the gospel of equality, and absolute affirmation of diversity are the baseline concerns. We should share and explore and ask questions together, and not be 'preachy,' or dogmatic or absolutizing about things.

Paul says to Timothy: remember judgment day, and preach the unadulterated Word to the church that you're in.

I find it interesting that there's no real mention of the sacraments in the Pastoral Epistles. It's not that they're unimportant. But there's no commendation here for indiscriminate baptisms to help bring outsiders in, and no focus on parish communion as the primary way to feed them.

*So many* of the silver bullets, the new and latest courses or conferences or techniques recommended by this group or that—the things which we're told will finally bring about change and sort out our problems and really make things start to grow... so many are more focused on *this* world, and making the church appear better in the eyes of our society, than concerned with the second coming of Christ and the proclamation of His Word.

Paul says, preach the Word.

Luther once wrote about those who hold the spoken Word in contempt. The lips of a minister, he said, 'are the public reservoirs of the church' because in them are stored the word of God. 'You see, unless the Word is preached publicly,' he said, 'it slips away. The more it is preached, the more firmly it is retained. Reading it is not as profitable as hearing it, for the live voice teaches, exhorts, defends, and resists the spirit of error. Satan does not care a hoot for the written Word of God, but He flees at the speaking of the Word.' Luther speaks about this 'live voice' of preaching, and how it 'penetrates hearts and leads back those who stray... it teaches the ignorant, it corrects those who err, it condemns those who corrupt it.'[3] But how many value preaching of the Word like this today?

So our strategy is to unleash the Word of God. Full stop. However you do it, wherever you do it, get the Word out. It's the only divinely-sanctioned strategy for the church that will have any impact on judgment day.

The *context of ministry* is the dangers and disappointments that come from engaging with real people in the real world. The *content of ministry* is the preaching of God's Word. But what else does Paul say about how we are to go about this ministry? What does he say, thirdly, about *the conduct of our ministry*?

---

3.   Martin Luther, *Luther's Works, Vol. 18: Minor Prophets I: Hosea-Malachi* (ed. Jaroslav Jan Pelikan, Hilton C. Oswald, and Helmut T. Lehmann; Saint Louis: Concordia Publishing House, 1999), p. 401 (on Malachi 2:7).

## The conduct of ministry

*How* are we to preach the Word? Some commentators say that 2 Timothy 4:2 contains five commands: preach, be ready at all times, reprove, rebuke, exhort. But I think it's better to see it as one command, unpacked. These are the ways we are to preach. So: preach the Word—*that is,* be ready at all times to reprove, rebuke, and exhort.

Because that's what preaching is. It's not 'explaining the Bible,' as some people say when they're introducing the sermon on Sunday mornings. 'Lee is now going to come and explain the Bible.' No, he's not. He's going to *preach* it to you. This is not going to be a nice informative little talk you can listen to and take or leave. I'm going to correct wrong ideas from the Bible; I'm going to rebuke wrong behaviour from the Bible; and I'm going to exhort and urge and try to move you, because the Bible is more than information. How you respond will have an eternal impact.

So get set, be ready, always on duty like a good solider of Christ. Opportunities to proclaim the Word may come along at any hour of the day or night, both in the pulpit and out of it. Be ready to take advantage of those chances to equip people for the appearing of Christ. It's not just nine to five, because it's not 'a job.' Paul expects us to be active, industrious, energetic in our Master's service, and not just when we're young; stewarding our time and energies responsibly of course, but being ready whenever we're needed (and whether we think it's going to go down well or not).

Notice too the different keys in which we have to play. There's both severity and kindness in 'reprove, rebuke and exhort.' John Stott suggests this is almost a classification of three different approaches to ministry: intellectual, moral and emotional. He says, 'For some people are tormented by doubts and need to be convinced by arguments. Others have fallen into sin, and need to be rebuked. Others again are haunted by fears, and need to be encouraged. God's word does all this and more. We are to apply it relevantly.'[4]

Like Luther, the excellent Reformation-era Archbishop of Canterbury, Edmund Grindal (1519–83), was a great advocate for the 'live voice' of freshly prepared, custom-applied preaching. That's because, as he said, 'Public and continual preaching of God's word is the ordinary mean and instrument of the salvation of mankind.' You cannot get more significant and exalted than that! Preaching is the normal way that people get saved, but it also has a number of other very positive spiritual effects. 'By preaching of God's word,' writes Grindal, 'the glory of God is enlarged, faith is nourished, and charity increased. By it the ignorant [person] is instructed, the negligent exhorted and incited, the stubborn rebuked, the weak conscience comforted.'[5] Good preaching does all this, because it's not just the transfer of data, of explaining facts and figures. Reformation theology has always exalted the urgent preaching and lively proclamation of the Word as a vital instrument of spiritual growth.

In the early church, John Chrysostom also made a good point about this. Thinking about 'convict, rebuke, encourage' he said that if we omit any of these, the others become useless. If we rebuke people without convicting and correcting them, they'll think we're just harsh and not really tolerate it. If we convince people, then they will submit to a rebuke; but if we don't, they will just remain headstrong. Similarly, he says, if we convict and rebuke, but only do it vehemently, without positive exhortations as well, all our labour will be lost. Because, 'conviction is intolerable in itself if consolation be not mingled with it.'[6]

---

4. John R. W. Stott, *Guard the Gospel: The Message of 2 Timothy* (Downers Grove, IL: InterVarsity Press, 1973), p. 108.

5. See Lee Gatiss, *Edmund Grindal: The Preacher's Archbishop* (London: Latimer Trust, 2013).

6. John Chrysostom, *The Homilies of S. John Chrysostom, Archbishop of Constantinople, on the Epistles of St. Paul the Apostle to Timothy, Titus, and Philemon* (Oxford; London: John Henry Parker; J. G. F. and J. Rivington, 1843), p. 251.

How are we to do all this? It says, 'with complete patience and teaching.' Or as the NIV translates it, 'with great patience and careful instruction.' Patience and care are needed because it's not just about the harshness of our rebukes or the precision of our doctrine. Sometimes we get too harsh or are too quick with correction and rebuke because we're impatient to see change in people. That's understandable and springs from a laudable motive. But Paul urges patience.

On the other hand, sometimes people simply don't get it—not because we're not rebuke-y enough, but because we're not clear enough. It's not our lack of passion and conviction in the pulpit that holds people back, but our lack of clarity in doctrine. So we need great patience *and* careful instruction.

Evangelicals may be tempted to a certain overconfidence here, thinking that we don't need to hear this as much as others do, because obviously we highly value 'careful teaching.' But I wonder if many of us are naturally quite slothful. If we are blessed with a modicum of talent or education, we can bluff our way through life, and essays at seminary, and writing sermons, and only do what we need to do. We don't value deep thinking and rigorous training as much as our forebears did and can often succumb to a supercilious anti-intellectualism which looks down on 'experts' as inevitably impractical and boring, and constantly devalues the knowledge of those who have thought more patiently and taught more carefully. Does this attitude have an impact on our ministry? Is there a rebuke here, even for us?

In their excellent and provocative book, *Bluffocracy*, James Ball and Andrew Greenway demonstrate how 'Britain became a bluffocracy.' They mean that we are led by people whose main acquired skill after years of education is surviving weekly 'essay crises' at university, through various deflecting tricks and tactics which mask their true ignorance and superficial grasp of their subject. This leads to 'the short-termism that fuels many of our country's political failures and scandals.' The problems with the way many of our senior leaders and civil servants have been trained is that they have been taught 'to confidently present an argument with little to no knowledge of the field at hand,' in a system which 'can create a dangerous sense of your own talent' and a 'constant overconfidence' that is corrosive of trust and credibility. As they conclude, 'Hardwired blagging is woven into the cause of many challenges we're facing, shaping the short-termism and lack of detail that plagues our national institutions, and contributing to the crisis of trust in British political life.' So what we get, they say, is 'ministerial amateurism.'[7] Is it just with political 'ministers' that this is an issue? I think not. Laziness and learning how to cut corners all the time can be a problem. But ministry is not a convenient lifestyle where that kind of approach is acceptable to the one who calls the shots.

Even if we are patient and careful and diligent, as the Reformer Martin Bucer (1491–1551) once pointed out, some people may only praise your sermons because they found them very applicable to someone else, the kind of person they like to hear criticized. All they take from our sermons is an excuse to run down those they don't like, rather than an opportunity to be warned or built up themselves.[8]

So the Lord's servant must be patient with people, because they are slow to learn and put things into practice. And because our congregations will always present us with what Milne calls 'an endless catalogue of needs.' Milne says, in a word to those of us in turnaround or revitalization situations without much of a history of evangelical ministry: 'The church is rarely reformed overnight, rather it succumbs to the patient toil, faithful witness and prayerful efforts of the man of faith. He must dependently wait for God to work

---

7. James Ball and Andrew Greenway, *Bluffocracy* (London: Biteback, 2018), pp. xi, 17, 24, 92, 77, 85.

8. Martin Bucer, *Concerning the True Care of Souls* (trans. Peter Beale; Edinburgh: Banner of Truth, 2009), p. 201, p. 196.

through his efforts, instead of forcing people to listen to him and do as he says, in the false belief that his own energies and commitment will carry the day.'[9]

Why so patient and careful? Because there is a great contest: a competition for ears. We want people to listen to the Word of God for the sake of their future happiness. But they would often rather gather for themselves a whole collection of teachers who will help them focus on their present desires. Our strategy for winning that aural competition is patient, persistent, precise preaching that corrects, rebukes and encourages.

Evangelical is as evangelical does. An axiom I (sort-of) learned from that great theologian, Forrest Gump. Evangelical is as evangelical does. An evangelical strategy for any kind of ministry must be first and foremost a strategy which focuses on proclaiming God's Word, with great patience and careful instruction. Whatever your strategy is, it's *not* an evangelical strategy if it's not about proclaiming the Word, in season and out of season: if it's always silent in the face of controversy, or if it relies on something else to accomplish its goals, or if it doesn't think faithful preaching is up to the job, or if it gives up too easily in the face of ignorance and opposition.

Ear ticklers will not endure 'sound doctrine,' Paul says. Sound or healthy doctrine is not about pleasing our desires. So our conduct of ministry must reflect the unpopular truth that it *can* be healthy to not pursue your desires, contrary to what the world says. The truth we should listen to is not about being true to ourselves, our passions, our base longings, although the myths which inspire our surrounding culture would say otherwise.

People who believe the myths told by the media and in education and the zeitgeist of our age will not endure sound teaching. They'll hate it, and oppose it, and scoff at it, and despise it. They'll have a sort of insatiable urge to

9.  Milne, *1 Timothy, 2 Timothy, Titus*, pp. 174–5.

grab all the 'spicy hits of information,'[10] which reinforce the stories they prefer to inhabit, building vast intellectual echo chambers, which tell them only what they want to hear, and magical mirrors, which reliably name them the fairest of them all, whatever they do. It's hard not to love a story like that, and hate any counter narrative.

We see that all around us in some of the big issues of the day in the Church of England and many other denominations. But you'll also see it in academic theology. I've noticed in academic theology that evangelicals always have to read and quote and footnote the liberal and unbelieving academics, in order to be taken seriously. We do the hard work of listening and refuting. But *they* hardly ever engage seriously with the best of evangelical theology and biblical studies. Don't be surprised if you have to work harder as an evangelical, but still aren't heard. It's not unusual. But be patient and diligent all the same.

In contrast to the conduct of false teaching, Paul tells Timothy in verse 5, 'As for you, always be sober-minded, endure suffering, do the work of an evangelist, fulfil your ministry.' Keep your head, because others don't. Just turn on the internet and you'll see. But you, take a step back. Cultivate that 'unruffled alertness,'[11] that commends the truth and thinks before it tweets. Endure hardship, because others won't. First sign of difficulty and they'll be tempted to give up and go home and look for a safer and easier environment to work in. Don't give up, just because it's hard.

Do the work of an evangelist. This is not just about making evangelism a priority, something it's hard for many clergy with busy parishes to do either for themselves or for their churches. Something which Timothy might be urged to do if his congregation was dwindling due to his

---

10.  See Stott, *Guard the Gospel: The Message of 2 Timothy*, p. 111 quoting Arndt-Gingrich.

11.  Donald Guthrie, *Pastoral Epistles: An Introduction and Commentary* (Downers Grove, IL: InterVarsity Press, 1990), p. 186.

insistence on sound teaching and his identification with the unpopular apostle. No, it's probably not as restricted in meaning as that, as Don Carson said in *Themelios* a few years ago.[12] It's about being a gospeller, who applies the good news of salvation in Christ to everything they do. It's about remembering we're not called to be managers or entertainers or cultural warriors or social commentators or TV personalities or moral instructors. It's our job to announce the good news of Christ at all times.

The fact that Paul calls for these specific things also shows what temptations we may have in the midst of the battle. But by doing these things, conducting our ministries this way rather than another way, we will show that we are true ministers of Christ, and fulfil our ministries, as Paul puts it. Paul himself is a good example of the 'conduct of ministry' he's commending. He is so ready in season and out of season that even in his prison cell he wants his books, and Mark who is so useful to him in ministry.

In chapter 3, he told Timothy to avoid charlatans and beware of them. And he is consistent in this when he invokes a curse on Alexander the coppersmith in 2 Timothy 4:14. 'The Lord will repay him according to his deeds.' The Lord will indeed repay the brazen and resolute malice of the most outspoken and determined antagonists of the gospel. But when it comes to those who desert him personally, out of fear or weakness, Paul prays 'May it not be held against them.'

And though *deserted* in prison and *defenceless* at his trial and so *destitute* he needs Timothy to bring him a cloak from 600 miles away—when everyone to whom he first gave the spiritual gift of the Epistle of Romans has abandoned him to his fate—he doesn't lose heart or perspective. He doesn't suddenly berate them for their ingratitude or give up in a

---

12. See D. A. Carson, 'Do the work of an evangelist,' in *Themelios* 39.1 (April 2014) at http://themelios.thegospelcoalition.org/article/do-the-work-of-an-evangelist, accessed Mar 3, 2024.

huff, as we might do when faced with the silly sheep in our flocks. No. May it not be charged against them.

Paul prays for those who didn't stand by him, even in his very last letter, as he faced the prospect of execution. Would you? Would you be that practised in sober patience and the endurance of suffering?

The *context of ministry* is that there will always be these struggles and stresses. So the *content of our ministry*, our strategy, should always be preaching the Word. Our *conduct of ministry* should be diligent, thoughtful, patient and sober-minded. These are our tactics in the midst of the battle.

But finally, there is also the consolation of ministry.

## The consolation of ministry

In verse 1, the eternal seriousness of the charge to be a preacher rests on the idea that Christ is watching right now and will one day assess our ministry. But Paul, having fought the good fight and finished his race, looks forward to a crown of righteousness, which the Lord will soon award him.

Nero, the unrighteous Caesar, may give him the thumbs down. But Christ, the righteous judge, will give him a crown of righteousness. You don't win such a crown by unrighteous methods or unrighteous behaviour. It's for those who have lived in the light of that eternal moment and been ever-conscious of the watchful eye of God. And it is for *all* who have loved His appearing; that is, all who will look back from the brink of eternity and say, as Christ returns, '*This* is what I've longed for and worked towards my whole life and ministry. This is what it was all about.'

When we see the crowns being given out on that day, will we feel regret? 'I wish I had known it was going to be like this! I was fooled into thinking ministry was about something else... an honourable and respected profession, a way of making a living for a few years, a way of pursuing social justice, in a world that was actually passing away. I wish I had realized. If only I'd known...'

Woe to us if we forget the coming of Christ in glory to judge the living and the dead! Woe to us if we love this present world more than the appearing of Christ and that world to come! Woe to us if we do not minister every day with that day of reckoning in mind!

But if we do... if that day is our real passion, we can be sure of the future. In his lonely prison cell, his Gethsemane moment, Paul can look to Jesus and the gospel. In the midst of his struggles, the Lord stands by him and strengthens him, he says. He never forgets his ambition to proclaim the gospel to the gentiles. And he trusts that whatever happens to his mortal flesh the Lord will rescue him from every evil deed and bring him safely to His heavenly kingdom.

We may not be saved on every occasion from every lion that we face. But if we keep going, and stick to the strategy and methods of Christ, who is coming to give out the crowns... no power of hell or scheme of man can ever pluck us from His hand, or take away the reward of a good and faithful servant.

This prayer from the first English-language ordination liturgy by Thomas Cranmer in 1549, is a good place to end our study of 2 Timothy:

> Most merciful Father, we beseech you to send down upon these your servants, your heavenly blessing, and so endue them with your Holy Spirit that they, preaching your word, may not only be earnest to reprove, beseech, and rebuke with all patience and doctrine, but also may be to such as believe a wholesome example, in word, in conversation, in love, in faith, in chastity, and purity, that faithfully fulfilling their course at the latter day, they may receive the crown of righteousness laid up by the Lord, the righteous judge, who lives and reigns, one God with the Father and Holy Ghost, world without end. Amen.[13]

---

13.   *The Form and Manner of Making and Consecrating Archbishops, Bishops, Priests, and Deacons* (1549), Consecrating of a Bishop.

# 7

# A Remedy for the Plague

## *Titus 1*

In England, we are going through difficult days in our church and in our country right now. Many commentators lament the lack of good leadership at the highest levels of government, the democratic deficit, and the horrendous paralysis of Parliament as we approach some of the most momentous months and years for our United Kingdom. The Western nations are led by some who prefer to do international diplomacy via social media, and others who pursue progressive virtue signalling rather than social stability and care for the poor, which should be their proper concerns.

Is the church in any better position? The Independent Inquiry into Child Sex Abuse has excoriated our bishops, our processes, and our institutional cover-ups. Senior evangelicals have been at the forefront of apostasy, abuses of power and appalling behaviour. There is little credibility left in the mantra of 'mutual flourishing,' which is undermined at every level by broken promises and empty assurances.

Some money and time has been put into reform and renewal programmes, but we continue to shrink, and to shirk our responsibilities to speak clearly to the nation about Jesus' gospel of repentance and forgiveness and the new life of obedience to the Spirit which He shows us in His Word. Rather, we are busy baptizing, sometimes literally, the deep confusions of our society about sexuality and gender. And few hear the message of the cross, warnings of hell, or the call of heaven.

During the Reformation, a committee overseen by Archbishop Thomas Cranmer produced a reformed canon law for the newly reformed Church of England. The church is in a mess, it declares. What do we need to do to sort it out? Here's what they said:

> Just as the condition of the state is ruined when it is governed by people who are stupid, demanding, and burning with ambition, so in these times the church of God is struggling, since it is committed to the care of those who are totally incompetent to assume so important a task, in which respect it has fallen very far short indeed of those rules of the blessed Paul, which he prescribed to Timothy and Titus. Therefore we must find an appropriate remedy for so serious a plague on our churches.[1]

More specifically, they continue:

> In a presbyter, there shall shine those qualities described by the Lord Paul in 1 Timothy 3 and in Titus 1. They shall regularly feed the flock of God committed to them with the word of life, and they shall constantly nurture all Christians in a sincere obedience both to God, and to the magistrates, and to those placed in a higher dignity, and earnestly encourage them to love one another. They shall not be drunkards, gamblers, fowlers, hunters, hypocrites, sluggards, or weaklings, but they shall devote themselves to the study of sacred letters, to the preaching of the Word, and to prayers to the Lord for the church.[2]

So, at a time when the people are languishing for lack of good leadership in the state, and torn apart by plots and divisions, the church must lead the way by recovering a vision of godly government and guidance. That was at the

---

1. Gerald Bray (ed.), *Tudor Church Reform: The Henrician Canons of 1535 and the Reformatio Legum Ecclesiasticarum* (Woodbridge: Boydell Press, 2000), pp. 280–1 (*Reformatio*, 11.1).

2. Bray (ed.), *Reformatio*, pp. 350–1 (20.4).

heart of the Reformation under Edward VI. And, I would contend, it must be at the heart of any efforts we hope to make today for the reform and renewal of our church. So let's examine the 'appropriate remedy for so serious a plague' in Paul's instructions to Titus. This is a God-breathed prescription to save the *church* from those who are 'stupid, demanding, and burning with ambition' and to show the world a better way.

Titus 1 tells us what the church lacks, who the church needs, and why the church needs them. There's a three-part sermon right there. But let me come at this a different way. If we look at the last section of this chapter first, we'll see what the context is for Paul's letter. So let's look at verse 10 onwards to start with, and try to discern what is going on in Crete. The situation Paul is writing into is that the church is unsettled, unhealthy and unfit.

## The church is unsettled, unhealthy and unfit

Paul tells Titus that the church needs godly leaders in verse 5. But from verse 10 onwards, he tells us why that is so important. 'For,' he says, 'there are many who are insubordinate, empty talkers and deceivers.' There are rebellious and unruly people on the island, spreading false teaching and idle babble in the church. There's a lot of pointless twittering, which is causing deep and profound trouble for Christian families. People who say one thing but mean another, or who clothe their false teaching in orthodox terminology so that the uninformed might be fooled.

These people must be silenced, says Paul, because they are upsetting whole families. The word for 'upsetting' doesn't just mean it's making a few people a bit unhappy. Sad face emoji. It's the word John uses in his Gospel when he describes what Jesus did to the moneychangers' tables. He upset them. He overturned them. He upended them. And that's what these insubordinate deceivers are doing to Christian families by their teaching.

They are teaching what they ought not to teach. And doing it for the sake of shameful gain—to line their own pockets with 'filthy lucre' as the King James Version translates this. But shameful gain could mean more than merely financial benefit. It's any kind of advantage or victory, but one here that is shameful. False teachers are making political and ecclesiastical progress in a way they should not be proud of, at the expense of the stability of Christian families. These people are liars, beasts and gluttons having given themselves over to sensuous pleasures rather than spiritual health—just like the rest of Cretan culture around them, it seems, which Paul illustrates with a song lyric from Cretan Top of the Pops.

Titus is told to rebuke them sharply so they may be *sound* in the faith—healthy in the faith. Because they are not healthy. Their minds and consciences are defiled, he says. Some of the language of purity and Jewish myths that Paul uses here, no doubt comes from the specific kind of false teaching being spread by the circumcision party. But don't be fooled; it's not just a dash of legalism. These people have 'devoted themselves to the commands of people who turn away from the truth,' and with that revolution in their thinking has come all kinds of nasty consequences.

So the church is unsettled and unhealthy, and in the final verse of the chapter he says these people are 'detestable, disobedient, [and] unfit for any good work.' This is in stark contrast to the faith that Jesus taught. Paul, it says at the top of the chapter, is a servant of Jesus Christ for the faith of God's elect and their knowledge of the truth. But these people have turned away from the truth. The gospel Paul teaches is a truth that leads to godliness. The errors of these detestable and disobedient people make them unfit for any good work. They think they're free with their insubordinate, disobedient approach to the faith. But their truth does not lead to godliness; it leads to the very opposite. To expand Epimenides, whom Paul quotes:

Liars always, men of Crete
Nasty brutes that live to eat
Overturning healthy rule
Replacing gospel food with gruel.[3]

So that's the sad situation in Crete. The details of the heresies upsetting the faith of some in ancient Crete are no doubt different to the specific errors floating about in our churches today. But it doesn't take too much of an imaginative leap to see what is making our church unsettled, unhealthy and unfit for purpose, does it?

So what is the 'appropriate remedy for so serious a plague'? Paul's answer is in verses 5-9. He says when the church is unsettled, unhealthy and unfit for purpose, what the church needs is leaders.

## The church needs leaders

We're not exactly sure when Paul visited Crete. But he realized at some point that the job was unfinished. Something important still needed to be done; it was an incomplete task. So he left his co-worker Titus there, specifically 'so that you might put what remained into order, and appoint elders in every town as I directed you.' There *were* Christian people there; in Titus 2 Paul calls them Jesus' very own people, and in Titus 3 he calls them 'our people.' But these believers needed proper organization and leadership.

This letter is written to Titus himself, but it is written to authorize him publicly for the task at hand, just as 1 Timothy and 2 Timothy were written not just for Timothy himself, but to prove to those he was ministering to that he had apostolic authority for the actions he was taking. Paul is very interested in establishing good leadership in churches.

So, contrary to what some people have alleged recently, Paul doesn't only ever write to congregations, such as the Ephesians or the Galatians. His letter to the Philippians for

---

3. The first two lines are from Jerome D. Quinn, *The Letter to Titus*, Anchor Bible 35 (New York: Doubleday, 1990), p. 107.

example is written to the saints at Philippi, '*with* the overseers and deacons' (Phil. 1:1). He was very much concerned with good order in the churches he pioneered. Indeed, from his first missionary journey onwards, the Apostle Paul set the pattern of appointing elders in the places where he planted churches, though not always straight away. So he goes to Antioch, Iconium and Lystra making disciples in Acts 13 and 14. Then at the end of Acts 14 he goes back through Lystra, Iconium, and Antioch appointing elders in each church. So, first comes making disciples through preaching the Word; together, those disciples form a church; and then elders are appointed in each church.

As the Elizabethan theologian Richard Hooker said, the church is a society, and it exists regardless of whether it gathers or not. He said,

> the Church is always a visible society of men, not an assembly, but a society. For although the name of the Church be given to Christian assemblies, although any multitude of Christian men congregated may be termed by the name of a Church, yet assemblies properly are rather things that belong to a Church. Men are assembled for performance of public actions, which actions being ended, the assembly dissolves itself and is no longer in being, whereas the Church which was assembled, does no less continue afterwards than before.[4]

So, when we gather, in twos and threes or hundreds, it is the *church* that assembles; it isn't the assembling that brings the church into being. Moreover, the church exists even if it doesn't have that council of elders, despite what Cyprian in the early church and some others say about the church being *in* the bishop.[5] But as Richard Hooker also says, the

---

4.   Richard Hooker (ed. McGrade), *Ecclesiastical Polity*, 1:145 (3.1.14).

5.   See Cyprian of Carthage, 'The Epistles of Cyprian,' in *Fathers of the Third Century: Hippolytus, Cyprian, Novatian, Appendix* (ed. Alexander Roberts, James Donaldson, and A. Cleveland Coxe, trans. Robert Ernest Wallis; vol. 5 of *The Ante-Nicene Fathers*; Buffalo, NY: Christian Literature Company, 1886; pp. 374–5 (Epistle LXVIII). cf. Ignatius, *Smyrneans*, 8-9 in Ignatius of Antioch, 'The Epistle of Ignatius to the Smyrnæans,' in *The Apostolic Fathers with Justin Martyr and Irenaeus* (ed. Alexander

apostles formed churches in all the places where the Word of God was received. And:

> All Churches by them erected, received from them the same Faith, the same Sacraments, the same form of public Regiment [that is, organisation or polity]. The form of Regiment by them established at first was, That the laity or people *should be subject* to a College of Ecclesiastical persons, which were in every such City appointed for that purpose. These in their writings they term sometimes Presbyters, sometimes Bishops.[6]

So Titus is to appoint elders in each town (not over each house-church, notice, but a council of elders for each town). Some of these would be overseers of domestic house-churches, with specific duties of leading and teaching in extended families. But not every elder would be a teacher-overseer (1 Timothy 5:17 perhaps draws a distinction). And not every house-church leader would necessarily be on the council of elders, otherwise Titus wouldn't need to discern and appoint.

The terms elder and overseer were not exactly synonymous, then, but they might overlap a bit in some contexts. There's a slightly awkward merging in the first century as the church grows, of the household pattern of overseer and deacon with a synagogue or community pattern of a council of elders.[7] So the Apostle Paul directs his delegate, Archbishop Titus, to appoint elder-overseers, presbyter-bishops, to lead the house-churches in each town on Crete, because that is what the church lacks, and badly needs in its unsettled and unhealthy state.

From other places, such as 1 Timothy, we learn that the elder-overseers may also have deacons working alongside

---

Roberts, James Donaldson, and A. Cleveland Coxe; vol. 1 of *The Ante-Nicene Fathers;* Buffalo, NY: Christian Literature Company, 1885), pp. 89–90.

6.   Richard Hooker, *Ecclesiastical Polity*, 3:81 (7.5.1) *my emphasis.*

7.   See Andrew D. Clarke, *A Pauline Theology of Church Leadership* (London: T&T Clark, 2008), pp. 52–60 or Roger Beckwith's *Elders in Every City* (Carlisle: Paternoster, 2003) for more on how this all developed.

them. Until this appointing of leaders is done, there is a key ingredient missing, something lacking in the church for its wellbeing and continuance. The church exists already without this. But it is better off with elders and overseers. To use the words of Cranmer's canon law: without this competent, qualified leadership, the church of God is struggling.

So apostolic order requires a council of Christian elders in a town (some of whom may be overseers with specific duties), with men such as Timothy and Titus having an archiepiscopal role over a wider field and supervisory powers over pay, discipline and ordination as we see in 1 Timothy 4, 5 and 6. Some of this was fairly fluid in the early days, of course, but as the *Book of Common Prayer* Ordinal summarizes this for us:

> It is evident unto all men diligently reading holy Scripture and ancient Authors, that from the Apostles' time there have been these Orders of Ministers in Christ's church; Bishops, Priests, and Deacons [overseers, presbyters or elders, and deacons]. Which offices were evermore had in such reverend estimation, that no man might presume to execute any of them, except he were first called, tried, examined, and known to have such qualities as are requisite for the same; and also by publick Prayer, with imposition of Hands, were approved and admitted thereunto by lawful authority.

What the requisite qualities are for such people, is precisely what Paul addresses next. Because, as Cranmer said, we don't want elders and overseers who are incompetent. So when the church is unsettled, unhealthy and unfit, the church needs leaders. Most of all, says Paul, the church needs godly teachers.

## Leaders must be godly teachers

Titus 1:6-9 tells us what kind of people should be appointed to leadership in the church. Not the kind of people who are 'stupid, demanding, and burning with ambition'—they are making a big enough mess of the state. No, what we need is godly teachers.

Only appoint elders in a town, says Paul, *if* you can find people like this: '*if* anyone is above reproach, the husband of one wife, and his children are believers and not open to the charge of debauchery or insubordination.' What we're looking for is someone of unquestioned integrity and consistency, someone of irreproachable character. Not perfect. It doesn't say you have to be perfect, because that's impossible of course. But if there's someone whose motives and actions and words are constantly suspect or inconsistent—that person is not to be appointed to any level of church leadership. You don't know what their real agenda is, but it probably won't be God's agenda.

Then it says an elder must be literally, 'a one-woman man.' That doesn't rule out singles, of course, it just means that if a church leader is married they must be *faithfully* married. Not a philanderer. Certainly not polygamous, as if that needed saying.

And they must have faithful children. I don't think Paul means 'faithful' here as in the children must all be sound converted believers 'or else.' But he is saying (as he says elsewhere) that if someone cannot run their own household very well then they should not be put in charge of God's household. If you have insubordinate children and you cannot handle them in a godly way, then how can you be entrusted with handling insubordinate and disobedient people in the churches?

So this is what people ought to be like if you're going to appoint them to the council of elders in a town. This is then unpacked for us in three ways. He tells us what a good minister should *not* be; what they *should* be; and what they should *do*.

Notice it turns to singular... *elders*, becomes '*an* overseer.' Some people have seen in that regular use of the plural for presbyters or elders and the singular for overseer or bishop, the start of the idea that one bishop will end up presiding or chairing the local college of presbyters. That is what generally happened as time went on, but whether it's what Paul intended or what God demands, I'll leave for discussion at another time.

The important thing is, what should an overseer be like? Look at the list of negatives in verse 7. They must not be: arrogant, or quick-tempered, or a drunkard or violent or greedy for gain. So we don't want someone who is overbearing, arrogantly thinking of themselves as superior to others and making sure everyone appreciates their greatness. They'll be too busy pointing out to people how wonderful they are, that they won't have time to point people to Jesus.

They should also not be quick-tempered. God is slow to anger, and as stewards of a patient God, it is important not to fly off the handle whenever someone makes a silly comment after your sermon or when something goes wrong.

Drunkards need not apply for the role of overseer. You can't reach for the whisky or run for the pub every night to drown your sorrows at the hard work of looking after God's people and trying to deal with detestable heretics. You don't deserve another bottle of wine because you're one of the sound crowd. Alcohol abuse leads to other kinds of abuse, however good the vintage, however singular the malt.[8]

An overseer must not be violent, as if Paul is saying, 'Look, Titus, I know how tempting it is to fight fire with fire. These evil beasts and lazy gluttons on Crete are a rum lot, and they can be quite pushy and unruly. But don't think to counter that by appointing pugnacious and demanding bullies as overseers. That kind of coercion and control will not further the faith of God's elect. Jesus gave *His* blood for the church—so no one should be shedding the church's blood with harsh treatment, however good they might be at preaching on a Sunday or writing blogs against the circumcision party.'

---

8. Alcohol *per se* is not entirely forbidden to elders of course, as 1 Timothy 5:23 makes clear.

An overseer should not be greedy for gain. Because that's what the false teachers are in it for, shameful gain. And while a worker is worth his wages, and 'double honour' in some cases, ministry in God's church is not a money-making profession. It's a sacrificial calling, with treasure in heaven for a good and faithful servant who seeks first the kingdom of God and 'the hope of eternal life.' It's about serving the Christ who Himself served us, by giving up the riches of heaven to die in poverty for our sake.

What a contrast here between the true overseer and the disobedient heretic.

But look also at the consistency of life that is demanded. Look at the list of positives in verse 8. The overseer must be 'hospitable, a lover of good, self-controlled, upright, holy, and disciplined.' That is, Titus, you want someone who has good relationships with people. They like people, not just ideas. They visit and have people round, rather than hiding away in their study. They have emotional intelligence and relational skills, because soft skills are useful in hard places, in a way that introverted book learning is not.

The kind of person we're looking for loves other people, and loves what is good. Because in the last days there will be people who are 'brutal, not loving good' (2 Tim. 3:3). Remember '[love] does not rejoice at wrongdoing, but rejoices with the truth' (1 Cor. 13:6) and we want our ministers to be drawn to 'whatever is true, whatever is honourable, whatever is just, whatever is pure, whatever is lovely, whatever is commendable' (Phil. 4:8). Whatever unforeseen things come their way, a person with a character like this will not go far wrong.

They must be 'self-controlled, upright, holy, and disciplined.' A measured temperament in a law-abiding citizen will stand out a mile in a place like Crete. Holiness and self-control will be distinctive in a society or church full of lazy liars on the lookout for filthy lucre. Church leaders must be mature Christian believers with mature Christian characters, living consistent, publicly unimpeachable lives.

If they're not—you're asking for trouble. Maybe not today. Maybe not tomorrow. But sooner or later, the shipwreck will come.

So this is what an overseer must not be. And what an overseer must be, if the church is to weather the inevitable storms.

But finally, Paul told us at the start of this letter that God, who never lies, promised eternal life to us through the preaching of His Word. So an overseer must hold firmly to that trustworthy Word, which was entrusted to Paul, and taught and passed on to us through the ages. They must be godly, and have a firm grip on that unchanging gospel. They don't just need *a* message to give people; they need *the* message.

Now, anyone who is at all intellectually engaged in their faith is bound to have questions and uncertainties of some sort. There are things about the faith and about the Bible and about creation that we may not quite understand. You may not have memorized Calvin's *Institutes*, and crossed every t and dotted every i. There are plenty of things I'm still chewing over in my mind about theology and philosophy and so on. But to be an overseer in God's church, we must hold firmly to the trustworthy Word as taught. We must trust God's unerring Word to lead us, and defer to it in every case of doubt or darkness. 'Every word of God is flawless; he is a shield to those who take refuge in him' (Prov. 30:5 NIV).

There are two reasons an overseer has to hold firmly to the trustworthy Word: so that they can give sound instruction, and so that they can detect and expose counterfeits.

If we don't hold firmly to such an anchor ourselves, we will never give sound instruction to those who rely on us for spiritually healthy food. A spiritually unhealthy, obese church full of evil beasts and lazy gluttons needs a decent diet. And we can't cook it up for ourselves: we need the trustworthy Word as it has been taught. If we're not confident in that God-given recipe, then we'll so easily be tempted to reach for the sugar that people like so much. Add too much salt, spice things up a bit, or pepper our sermons to make them seemingly more palatable.

So an overseer must hold firmly to the Father's recipe, in order to serve people healthy doctrine, to make them fit again. But also, note, finally we must hold firmly to the trustworthy Word, so that we can rebuke those who contradict it because those unsettling heresies troubling the church need to be silenced, says Paul. They must be rebuked and brought back to the truth they have turned away from. We must feed the sheep, but also defend them from wolves.

The church has always known this is an essential part of gospel ministry. We can't simply affirm everything; there must be denials too. It's no good saying in a Creed that Jesus is begotten of the Father, if we don't add that He is also 'not made.' We must close up the loopholes which the insatiable moths of sin and error try to chew open in the glorious tapestry of God's truth. Wherever they are nibbling away at the fabric, there we must be careful to deny them access.

In the seventeenth century, the Westminster Assembly of Divines got together and drew up their famous confession and catechisms. They also produced what's known as the Westminster Directory of Public Worship, giving directions on how to lead various church services. Their advice on preaching is well worth noting. They also add this, on refuting those who oppose the truth:

> In confutation of false doctrines, [the preacher] is neither to raise an old heresy from the grave, nor to mention a blasphemous opinion unnecessarily. But if the people be in danger of an error, he is to confute it soundly, and endeavour to satisfy their judgments and consciences against all objections...

> In dissuading, reprimanding, and publicly warning people (which requires special wisdom), let [the preacher], as there shall be cause, not only [expose] the nature and greatness

of the sin, with the misery attending it, but also show the danger his hearers are in to be overtaken and surprised by it, together with the remedies and best way to avoid it.[9]

So we're not to be like Thomas Aquinas. You may know the story of how one day in 1269, the great medieval theologian was having dinner with King Louis IX of France, and he wasn't really paying much attention to his royal companion. He was 'rapt out of himself' and spent most of the meal pondering the Manichees (a religious sect from the third century). All of a sudden, he emerged from his reverie, banged the table, and shouted, 'That settles the Manichees!' He called for his secretary to come and take some notes on his thoughts.[10]

No, don't get lost in your own little world, and drag up old heresies from the grave for no reason, just to show how clever you are at refuting them. And you don't necessarily need to unsettle your congregation with tales of all the grisly and appalling ways in which your sermon text this Sunday has been mauled by the heretical books they made you read at college. However, if you know that there is an actual and imminent risk of them falling for a dodgy interpretation of this passage or a doctrinal implication badly drawn from it, you must carefully and prayerfully show them the truth. If there is a real and present danger of them falling into some sin, which our culture encourages or the wider church seems to wink at, it is your God-given task to wisely warn them off, and show them how to avoid it. You're not properly shepherding the sheep if you don't protect them from the wolves, in a way that is gentle, not violent, and self-controlled, not arrogant.

---

9. See Gatiss and Green (eds.), *1-2 Thessalonians, 1-2 Timothy, Titus, Philemon*, p. 277. cf. *The Westminster Directory of Public Worship: Discussed by Mark Dever and Sinclair Ferguson* (Fearn: Christian Focus, 2008) which includes the text of the Directory as well as some edifying discussion.

10. Brian Davies, *The Thought of Thomas Aquinas* (Oxford: Clarendon Press, 1993), p. 8.

So this is the profile picture Paul gives Titus of someone who is suitable for ministry in the church at Crete. It is a portrait of the kind of person we desperately need in all our churches today.

Before I finish, I want us to particularly notice one very important thing. Titus is not told to look out for gifted people. He is not told to appoint people who have great leadership potential and sparkling oratory. Paul doesn't say pick some people from the best families and the best universities on Crete, and fashion them into instruments for transforming Cretan society. Titus is told to pick people whose character and commitment to the truth mark them out already as ambassadors for 'the truth which leads to godliness' because Paul knows that exalting gifts and charisma over character and deep commitment would leave the church open to manipulative mercenaries and narcissists. We've had enough of them—their shameful defections, their moral compromises, their abuses of power.

I don't have to name them. You know who they are.

So, we don't exalt gifts over godliness and a grip on the gospel. We don't exalt charisma over character and commitment. I know that 1 Timothy 3 says an overseer must be 'able to teach.' But that isn't a command to find people with teaching gifts and skills, or knowledge and degrees, and appoint them. Ability to teach is about more than didactic pedagogic technique. It's also about having such a firm grip on the gospel that consistency of life and clarity of teaching flow out of someone naturally and inevitably. This is why Martin Bucer says, in his book on *The True Care of Souls* that,

> churches have not taken their ministers from the same type of person as far as outward things are concerned: because God has not distributed his gifts in this way. He does not look upon the person: indeed, in order that it may be seen that all Christians, high and low alike, are nonetheless one in Christ, ministers of the church have been taken from people of high, middle or lower classes, as each was found

to excel in the necessary gifts for the care of souls... the Lord desires to have a group of people involved in the ministry of the church and uses many different sorts of people in it, who also come from all classes and are of all types.[11]

So I don't care how talented someone is, how passionate, how entrepreneurial, how attractive and clever or social media savvy. It doesn't matter what their educational, class, or family background is. That's not what we're looking for in the next generation of church leaders. The most important, but often ignored, word in this whole chapter is the first word of verse 6 (in the Greek or the ESV). Titus is told to appoint people as elders *if* and only *if*, he can find people who match this description here.

We're not seeking for those who can make an impressive career in the church, 'the ones to watch.' Rather, we're to be on the lookout for those who are trustworthy and true. Because we're not after sparkling celebrities, but faithful stewards of the gospel, and loyal servants of God.

I know it sounds mundane. But it's harder than you think to be this subversively counter-cultural in our leadership selection. Yet this is how we change *everything*.

So next time you hear someone complaining about the current crisis, about how 'the condition of the state is ruined when it is governed by people who are stupid, demanding, and burning with ambition,' as Cranmer's church law put it, remember that the church is struggling too. It is unsettled, unhealthy and unfit in many ways. The church needs better leaders. The church needs godly teachers.

Your mission, should you choose to accept it, is to be the change we want to see in the church. That's the first step to changing the world.

---

11. Bucer, *The True Care of Souls*, pp. 56, 59.

# 8

# What Accords with Sound Doctrine

## *Titus 2*

What causes should I devote myself to? What should I give my time, talents and treasure to, if I want to really make a difference in this world? These are common questions, particularly for teenagers and young adults in the early stages of their working lives—that is, before they hit middle age like me and begin thinking about their pensions. As we learn about the world and try to find our niche in it, work out what we're here for, it's natural to ask: what can I do, to make a real impact? It's also a question many middle-age people ask, as they enter the 'second act' of their lives and wonder if there is more they could do in this world than their current day job which has paid the bills so far.

The world has various causes that it would like us to join: causes such as environmentalism, anti-racism, the redistribution of wealth, or maybe the revolutionary overturning of 'the elites.' We're invited to consider 'sticking it to the man' (and it usually is a man), to those in authority. We are urged to purify ourselves of attitudes from 'the wrong side of history,' and to cleanse ourselves of the people who promote them. De-platform! De-fund! De-colonize! These are the great causes which will vie for your attention on social media. The great righteous crusades of the moment. How dare you not get involved, and give yourself heart and soul to the movement?

Titus 2 is seemingly very mundane compared to that. Yes, Titus 3 will tell us how to behave towards the authorities—but not in the way you might think. But Titus 2 has nothing to say about environmentalism, Black Lives Matter, communism, the NHS, trans-rights or feminism as such. There's nothing here about making your nation great again, draining the swamp, levelling up, or anything like that either. Yet Titus 2 tells us about God's own great cause. And it invites us to join this cause, for the glory of God and the good of His world.

To join God's cause will mean going up against powerful vested interests. It will mean engaging potent cultural forces and entrenched opinions. It will be a struggle every day. But a powerful leader is provided—our God and saviour Jesus Christ—and a glorious vision of the future is promised, our blessed hope, when He comes again.

But that's not the way everyone sees things here. Some people have looked at Titus 2 and rather scoffed. It's all very bourgeois, isn't it? So boringly middle-class, this list of good behaviours. Verse 5 says the young women should be 'self-controlled, pure, working at home, kind, and submissive to their own husbands'—and why? So that 'the word of God may not be reviled.' This is how you do virtue signalling in first-century Crete, where Titus is. Teach them to be good little housewives. So people won't be nasty about our religion. So we can keep the show on the road for a bit longer.

And the men? Well, same thing. Be self-controlled, and, Titus—teach nicely with 'sound speech that cannot be condemned, so that an opponent may be put to shame, having nothing evil to say about us.' Behave nicely, like decent well-spoken members of Cretan society, so no one will say anything bad about us all.

And the slaves? They're told not to argue back to the masters, or nick their stuff, 'so that in everything they may adorn the doctrine of God our Saviour.' Make Christianity look good in the eyes of Cretan society. Conform to the expectations of the culture around us so that it will stop criticizing us. And maybe it will even want to join us.

Some people call this idea 'missionary accommodation'— live like the culture around you in order to reach it or to survive. Signal your virtue in terms the world understands, so they won't hate you.

The implication is that the things taught here in Titus 2 are not universal and for all time. They simply reflect the moral climate and cultural mores of that particular time and place. We can and should change how we behave as Christians, as our culture changes.

My wife and I were at a church service somewhere midweek a few years ago. It wasn't at our own church but somewhere else. The lectionary readings were from Leviticus and Titus 2. There was a young ordinand preaching. Well, not preaching, but giving a gloss on each reading as we went along. After Leviticus he told us and the young audience how important it was that God gave us rules to live by. Rules are very important he said. They tell us how to live. This was the message of the Old Testament lesson.

Later, someone read Titus 2. The ordinand then told us that if we were to follow the teaching of this reading, we should actually ignore some of the things it said because they are wrong now. Our culture is different, so we don't follow the things it says here anymore, if *we* want to live in a way that is acceptable and respectable to *our* culture.

So the Old Testament is good, giving us rules to live by. And the New Testament is... out of date with its rules, which we are free to abandon if they don't suit our culture anymore. There was no sense of irony at all. And no prizes for guessing which bits he thought were out of date. It wasn't the bit about being sober-minded or doing good works or not stealing from work. My wife had an interesting conversation with him afterwards, about how he had basically told her in his talk, that her whole life is a waste of time, because loving your husband and children and being busy working in the home is apparently passé now, and not what God wants.

I don't know if his encounter with a fearsomely intelligent and theologically well-educated woman will have changed his mind or not. But I do pray for that ordinand. Because he is going to find it hard in ministry working out what to say to people each week, when modern morality seems to change every time you refresh your Facebook feed. If we are motivated by a desire to accommodate to the world so that it will be nice to us, then that's what we are committing ourselves to. We are asking the world to set the agenda for us, giving it authority over the church and permission to dole out our marching orders as it sees fit.

Call me an old fundamentalist, but I just can't believe that the man who said in Titus 1 that Cretans are always liars, evil beasts and lazy gluttons is really telling us in the very next chapter that the church should accommodate its morality to whatever suits its surrounding, changeable culture. Just so that people will be nice about us and we can get along? Isn't *that*, rather, what the false teachers in Crete were doing? Paul says those false teachers had 'devoted themselves' to 'the commands of people who turn away from the truth' (Titus 1:14). What does Paul say at the end of Titus 1? 'They profess to know God, but they deny him by their works. They are detestable, disobedient, unfit for any good work.'

I think it's much more likely, therefore, that in Titus 2, Paul is saying this: Don't be like that. 'But as for you…,' he says, be different to the world. Live out the gospel, and *that* will stop any slander, as people will see it's an attractive lifestyle and that you are consistent with your principles. That's the main issue. Life and lip must go together. So walk the walk, not just talk the talk. People appreciate consistency, even if they don't live like that themselves. *Especially* if they don't live like that themselves. And the gospel produces a lifestyle in believers that is truly beautiful and magnetic—especially in a society like first-century Crete which thought that highway robbery was a noble pursuit (as Cicero put it).[1] A gospel lifestyle is the opposite of a carnal, cruel, Cretan lifestyle dominated by pragmatism and misdirected zeal.

What's happening here, in the two different readings of this chapter which I've talked about, is that the cultural accommodation idea is over-reading the *hina* clauses in verses 1-10. *Hina* is one of the Greek words for 'so that.' It's there in verses 5, 8 and 10. It's all *'so that* the word of God may not be reviled,' and *'so that* an opponent may be put to shame, having nothing evil to say about us,' and *'so that* in everything they may adorn the doctrine of God our Saviour.'

But those *hina* clauses are not giving us the ultimate reasons and motivations for living in the ways outlined in these verses. They tell us some of the *fruits* of living that way. But if we make it all about living in a way that outsiders won't revile you, we will make it all about the moving target of the culture around us, and we will overlook some things in this chapter that are even more important than a good reputation. Because verse 1 is more important, and so is the hinge of this chapter in verse 11. That's where the real engines are located in this chapter. That's where we find out the real motivations for joining 'the cause.'

### Healthy doctrine, healthy life

Let's look at verse 1 and verses 11 onwards, under two headings. The first point is in verse 1. It says healthy doctrine, healthy life.

Verse 1 says 'But as for you, teach what accords with sound doctrine.' Everything that Paul says in the next nine verses is an exposition of what that means. He tells us what kind of lifestyle matches sound doctrine. Because healthy doctrine leads to healthy lifestyles, just as surely as an unhealthy diet leads to an unhealthy body. Eating Mars

---

1. Mounce, *Pastoral Epistles*, 418 quoting Cicero, *Republic*, 3.9.15.

Bars all day and never getting any exercise will have an inevitable effect on your physical wellbeing. That diet is not in accord with a healthy lifestyle. Some of us have to learn this the hard way.

And it's a hard lesson to learn spiritually too. Doctrine is not an abstract thing. It's not amoral, and it's certainly not immoral. It has practical effects, whether you can see and spell out the experiential implications of every nuance in your doctrine or not. Each rock of doctrine creates ripples of real-world reactions when you throw it into the church. That's why we have to get our doctrine right, because it really matters on the ground.

After all, how you interpret a *hina* clause can make the difference between being a liberal who encourages people to discard bits of the Bible they find culturally inconvenient, thus splitting the church and undermining the apostolic faith by exchanging biblical morality for the latest bandwagon—or, being a faithful minister who encourages the men and women in your church to live their everyday lives in a way that pleases God. Big difference, from misinterpreting a single Greek word! So how much more important is it to get the even bigger doctrinal issues right, such as the doctrine of the Trinity, the authority of Scripture, Christology, Ecclesiology, Eschatology? Who knows what craters of ignorance and immorality it might create in the church if we are not clear and correct about those doctrines?

Teach what accords with sound doctrine, says Paul. Because doctrine must be fleshed out, and applied in concrete situations. And because we mustn't think it's obvious to everyone. It needs spelling out; the dots need to be connected. A misshapen ministry of all doctrine and no application will lead to misshapen Christians in the pews. As Calvin says in his sermon on this: 'God has not given us his word simply that it might beat against our ears, and for us to let whatever we hear slip away into the air. But he wants us to find pasture there and that our lives might be regulated by it and, to sum it up, that we should show by our deeds that we have not wasted our time being taught in his school.'[2]

Theological college or seminary is a great place to learn the doctrine. *And* to learn how it applies. You can't learn the theory in isolation from the practice. Because they go together. I hope that if you ever find yourself studying theology at such an institution, you'll be encouraged in your time there to always consider the implications of what you're learning. But college should also be a place where we learn how to *teach* these things. Because that's what this passage is saying. Yes, the congregations on Crete are reading this letter over Bishop Titus's shoulder. Paul knows they will see it and hear it too. But it is also a letter to Bishop Titus himself, reminding him of his task. He needs to teach people about these connections. Ministers need to develop the skills not just to know the truth, but to teach sound doctrine and everything that is in harmony with it and leads from it.

Titus 2:15 says he is to declare, exhort and rebuke, and let no one disregard what he is teaching. That's not easy to do. We need all the help and advice we can get on how to teach in such an effective way that people will actually listen. As you can see, we all need to work at that. I mean, how do you teach this chapter without it simply becoming a new stone tablet of dos and don'ts—a legalistic list of moral directives? Ponder that as we see Paul modelling it for us. Does he declaim against everybody's sins in a high-handed, self-righteous tone? Ponder his teaching method.

But what is it that accords with sound doctrine, in this passage? Notice what Paul does. He joins the dots for four groups of people, and for Titus himself. He talks to older men, older women, younger women and younger men. And he also speaks to Titus himself. Let's just unpack some of the detail.

---

2.  Gatiss and Green, *1-2 Thessalonians, 1-2 Timothy, Titus, Philemon*, pp. 283–4.

Everyone is told to be self-controlled in this passage. It's repeated so we don't miss it. Here's the point: sound doctrine will produce self-control. Lack of self-control means there's a doctrinal issue somewhere.

Paul is a pastor, so he also addresses each group of people in ways distinctive to them. Not to *each and every individual situation* with all its eccentricities and exceptions; but there's something particular in each application. So, men are to be sober-minded, dignified, sound in love and steadfastness. Because imagine a man who is the opposite of those things... Imagine an older man who lacks dignity, and is frivolous and silly. Imagine an older man whose mind is flighty and easily intoxicated, who is aloof and unloving, and who can't stick at anything. More than that, one who is content to be such a man. If that is what a Christian looks like, it won't commend the gospel. How can we teach older men to be more like the description Paul gives?

A few years ago I had the joy of being a consultant for Regent College Vancouver, with regards to their library of rare sixteenth- and seventeenth-century books. Many of them were donated to Regent by Jim Packer, whom I was privileged to know over many years. One of these old books was a seventeenth-century commentary on Titus by Thomas Taylor, parts of which I subsequently included in my Reformation Commentary on Scripture volume on the Pastoral Epistles. I recommended many of these books should be digitized, so you can probably read this online on their website. Thomas Taylor (1576–1632) says this about Titus 2:2:

> Why is soundness of faith required particularly of old men, being a grace that everyone, young as well as old, must strive for? Because they have had the use of the word longer, and therefore their profit should be answerable to their means. . . . Every man must labor to recompense the decay of nature with increase of grace: the weakness of the

body with soundness of mind; the failing of the outward man with the fortifying of the inward.[3]

This, I'd like to say, is a very good description of Dr Packer himself. Even into his nineties, when he was even more frail and physically weak than usual, he retained not just a healthy sense of humility and humour, but an active love for God and His Word, and a very healthy desire to continue learning and growing. I found that even more inspiring, almost, than his many excellent books and articles. He was the greatest Anglican theologian of our age, and he exemplified Titus 2:2. Sound in faith, if not in body for much of his life.

Older *women* are to be reverent, not slanderers or slaves to much wine. Imagine older women who are the opposite of that. They give in to every urge to gossip or glug. Will they train the younger women in the church in what is good? I find it interesting that the words for sober-minded, and this warning against drunkenness are attached to older men and women, not younger ones, who we might more naturally assume are the ones out on the town of an evening, overindulging. But no. As Thomas Taylor said, 'this age [old age] being full of infirmity, a cold and dry age, it is more desirous to strengthen, warm, and moisten itself with wine and strong drink, and without great watchfulness, easily overshoots itself.'[4] The Word warns us what to watch out for.

Imagine *younger* women who *don't* think loving their husbands and loving their children and being busy about the place is an important calling. Imagine if they are not kind, but harsh? Will this lead to harmonious marriages in the Cretan church where Titus is, or in your church for that matter? False teaching in Crete was 'upsetting whole families,' we were told, and making people rebellious. What is the effect of that teaching over the years? What will

---

3.  Gatiss and Green, *1-2 Thessalonians, 1-2 Timothy, Titus, Philemon*, p. 286.
4.  Gatiss and Green, *1-2 Thessalonians, 1-2 Timothy, Titus, Philemon*, p. 286.

people say about this Christianity lark, if that's the culture in church circles?

What do we have to do for people to live like this, in accord with sound doctrine? Well, after telling Titus that younger Christian men should be self-controlled (and work on that, because it's the one big thing he tells them), he urges Titus to be their role model. Because healthy doctrine has to lead to healthy lifestyles in us, the teachers, too. If we are in all respects a model of good works, if our teaching shows integrity, dignity and sound speech that cannot be condemned—that will lead the way.

Imagine a Titus, a minister, a bishop, who was the opposite of this, whose teaching did not have integrity because it wasn't in accord with the doctrine they pledged to uphold at their ordination or consecration. Imagine a bishop without dignity, who sounded off on social media without a second thought and alienated half their congregation with their ill-judged words. Imagine a curate who lampooned and larked around and slandered others in a Facebook or WhatsApp group. What effect would that have? Imagine an evangelical incumbent whose life was not in every respect a model of good works. What would people say about the church?

Paul says there should be sound speech, 'so that an opponent may... have nothing evil to say about *us*.' It's plural there. In other words, when church leaders teach badly and behave badly, it affects not just them, but all of us. Don't you feel that? Don't you feel that with the church today? Even in the evangelical part of the church today. Where some of us have not lived as Titus is here urged to live, it has had an impact on all of us. There can be accusations that we are *all* like that. People assume the worst, and they extrapolate.

The more I see of what goes on, in every part of the church, the more personally painful it can be. As Calvin says somewhere, a true and genuine pastor looks upon the sins of others not with finger-wagging but with grief. 'Nevertheless we must put up with many things which we are unable to correct,' he says, 'and if we cannot remedy them we should weep.'[5] He adds, 'Even so this is no excuse for us to leave God's church on the grounds that all are not living as they should.' Indeed, when he was commenting on 2 Corinthians 12:21, he wrote that Paul,

> lets us know the disposition of a true and genuine Pastor, when he says that he will look upon the sins of others with grief. And, undoubtedly, the right way of acting is this—that every Christian shall have his Church inclosed within his heart, and be affected with its maladies, as if they were his own,—sympathize with its sorrows, and bewail its sins... It is, indeed, a thing that is common to all the pious, to be grieved in every case in which God is offended, and to bewail the ruin of brethren, and present themselves before God in their room as in a manner guilty, but it is more particularly requisite on the part of Pastors.[6]

Paul continues with his instructions: Bondservants, slaves, are to be submissive to their masters, to do a good job, and not steal stuff from work. Because imagine a servant who became a Christian and then lived like that still. What would the master think about this new religion, Christianity? But imagine a slave who became a Christian and then started being an even better worker. Would that not adorn the doctrine of God our saviour?

Just a moment to pause there, since we've got here a mention of slavery. I realize that in our current cultural moment, this could be problematic. Paul doesn't advocate for the abolition of slavery here, so perhaps we ought to no-platform him and burn our Bibles, tear down the statues of Paul and smash his stained-glass windows? I think that would be unfair. But some people can suck venom even

---

5. John Calvin, *Sermons on 2 Timothy* (Edinburgh: Banner of Truth, 2018), p. 217.

6. John Calvin, *Commentaries on the Epistles of Paul the Apostle to the Corinthians* (Bellingham, WA: Logos Bible Software, 2010), pp. 389–90.

from the most wholesome food, as Calvin put it.[7] So let's think about how to address this concern.

Slavery was not a racial thing in the first-century world. It was not the same as slavery in the Southern United States in the nineteenth century, a black and white thing. We should be clear on that. Yet it's still not a pleasant thought, is it? So what do we do with verses about slaves?

The things asked of bondservants here are right for any working situation, and that's why they are asked of slaves. But slavery itself is not being taught as a norm, like other relationships. For instance, marriage is there in creation and in Ephesians 5 as a picture of Christ and the church. For the relationship of parents and children there is the fifth commandment and Ephesians 6, for example. But Paul doesn't appeal to anything like that for the institution of slavery. Where it exists, the morality urged of Christian slaves is the same as required for any Christian worker. But Paul never says 'You're a slave because that's what God wants. So deal with it.' Indeed, Paul encourages Christian bondservants to leave that state if they legally can (1 Cor. 7:21), and encourages Philemon to free Onesimus. But he tells slaves how to live in this present age, if they are Christians. Not that slavery is inherently right and good.

## Grace both saves and trains us

But here's the rub: what Paul is doing in this chapter so far is showing what kind of lifestyle accords with healthy doctrine. That's the point of all this. And the *ultimate* reason for all of these nitty-gritty applications is not to do with those Greek *hina* 'so that' clauses. It's ultimately all down to the Greek word *gar* in verse 11. The word 'for' is the hinge of this chapter. If we look at verses 1-10 in isolation, maybe we can focus too much on the idea that healthy gospel living should stop people saying bad things about the church. But

---

7.    John Calvin, *Commentary on the Gospel according to John* (Bellingham, WA: Logos Bible Software, 2010), p. 277 (on John 6:66).

if we put those verses into the context of the chapter as a whole, it is much clearer what is going on.

Basically, Paul says, 'teach what accords with sound doctrine... to these various groups of people, so their behaviour adorns the gospel since it's in accordance with the gospel... *because...*' ...and there are two reasons in verses 11-14. Two great motivations for teaching gospel living. Verses 11-14 tell us why we should live like verses 1-10, and it's not because we need to accommodate ourselves to our culture. They are the theological fuel that drives healthy gospel living. Paul says that Jesus came to redeem *and* to purify, and so the grace that saves us also trains us.

Now obviously verses 11-14 deserve a whole sermon, or a whole series of sermons, on their own. I have expounded them a bit more in a chapter in my book *The Forgotten Cross*.[8] But my primary focus here has been on the main flow of this whole chapter. Because I wanted to show how it anchors its lifestyle imperatives to healthy doctrine, rather than to the cultural mores of one particular place and time.

And that is clear from a brief look here, isn't it? So why teach what accords with sound doctrine? Because the grace which saves all kinds of people (men, women, old, young, slave, free), also *trains* them. It doesn't take us as we are and leave us that way. It moves us, impels us, drives us, trains us 'to renounce ungodliness and worldly passions'—such as those we've talked about: drunkenness, irreverence, unkindness, lack of integrity, undignified behaviour, argumentativeness, stealing. Those are ungodly, and indulge mere worldly desires such as everyone in our surrounding culture might indulge.

Grace teaches us to say no to those things, and yes to 'self-controlled, upright, and godly lives in the present age.' That general description 'self-controlled, upright, and godly' applies to all the things we've seen in this passage. It means it is godly for older men to be sound in faith, in love,

---

8. Lee Gatiss, *The Forgotten Cross: Some Neglected Aspects of the Cross of Christ* (Darlington: Evangelical Press, 2014), pp. 77–91.

in steadfastness. It is godly in general for older women to teach younger women to be submissive to their husbands and be busy working at home. This is an appropriate lifestyle that pleases God in this present age. This is how the gospel applies to our relationships, our religion and our responsibilities in this present age.

But there is also an age to come. And this is also what is meant to motivate our behaviour. We are waiting for our blessed hope, the appearing of the glory of our great God and saviour Jesus Christ. What a God and saviour He is! He is glorious and great, and yet His glorious greatness is revealed most in the first five words of verse 14. He gave Himself for us.

He was great and glorious and yet He gave Himself up for foul, smelly sinners like us. He is our blessed hope, and yet He gave Himself up for those who were not sound in faith, not sober, not submissive, not self-controlled. He gave Himself up precisely to redeem us from all that lawlessness. He gave Himself up, intending to purify for Himself a people who were anything but pure to start with. His purpose was to create a people—an elect people, as Titus 1:1 puts it—who are zealous for good works.

So the incarnation, the atonement, the resurrection, the ascension and the second coming of Christ are all focused on getting us to renounce ungodliness, be redeemed from lawlessness, and purified from our sin. The only thing which could possibly be in accord with such doctrine, then, is to live a life of good works. And that's what Titus 2:1-10 describes. So if we reject or neglect or ignore any of those lifestyle points in those verses, we are missing something about the incarnation, the atonement, the resurrection, the ascension and the second coming of Christ.

Our good works are not driven by our culture's definition of what is good and right and true. Worldly morality is so often driven by guilt, these days. A lot of the anti-racism rhetoric at the moment is about trying to make people feel guilty, even for things they have not personally done. But

Paul drives us by grace. I believe there is racism in our society (including much hidden antisemitism), and I believe there is such a thing as 'white fragility' which doesn't like to talk about it and gets defensive. But I don't think critical race theory has the answer to it. Only the gospel does.

A lot of the green agenda in the world is driven by fear. Many economic agendas are fuelled by greed. So much of our politics is characterized by anger, and division, and hatred. The response is not to take refuge in self-interest, but to be trained by grace to change. Grace teaches us a better way, and teaches us *in* a better way. It doesn't beat us up or bind us. It liberates and loosens.

The gospel of grace does have things to say about caring for our planet, about the vile sins of racism, about how to share our wealth, about dealing with our class differences, and how to care for those who are different. The world is not wrong to see those as areas of concern. But it needs the gospel to be brought to bear on those issues, because it alone has the real answer. We need grace to save us and train us, rather than letting the world set our agenda and dictate our tactics.

Those who repent and believe the gospel are not dirty and stained, but purified by Christ. We are not controlled or defiled by sin anymore. We do good works on that basis— not to purge ourselves of guilt and shame, or try to earn God's favour, but because we have already been forgiven. The gospel is not shaming others by exposing them and no-platforming them and trolling them on social media until they give in to your demands. The gospel is about living for the one who gave Himself up for us, being good, so they are ashamed to behave like that towards us.

Tell people that. This is far better than the message they're getting from false teachers or from our cancel culture. The gospel is the best cause in the world. So let's give them grace, and tell the world about our great God and saviour, Jesus Christ.

# 9

# The Mercy and Grace of God
## *Titus 3*

The Pastoral Epistles are particularly addressed to pastors, obviously, by a seasoned pastor missionary church planter and apostle: Paul. So they are peculiarly appropriate letters to study for anyone who is either considering full-time paid ministry, or training for it, or actively engaged in it.

In Titus 1, we learn the remedy for the plague which is undermining our churches. Not the coronavirus, which sadly has been a cause of terrible problems for us all, but the pandemic of poor pastoring, which upsets whole families and fills the church with untruth and ungodliness. We see in that opening chapter that when the church is unsettled, unhealthy and unfit, what it needs is godly teachers. In Titus 2, we are made to think about what it means to be committed to God's cause in the world, rather than merely virtue-signalling to the culture around us. We hear that healthy doctrine leads to a healthy community life, and that Christians are not motivated by guilt or fear in the way we live, as people often are by worldly campaigning; but we are motivated by the goodness of God and the grace of the gospel.

Here, in Titus 3, the apostle to the Gentiles turns his attention particularly to how we are to interact with the world around us, especially the unbelieving world and the powers and authorities placed over us. He often does this:

after talking about the good news of Jesus, he speaks about how Jesus' followers should behave towards one another in the light of it—in marriages, in families, in workplace relationships; and then he writes about how we face those outside the church in our wider communities. The gospel he preached was applied to both sets of relationships. You can see that pattern in Ephesians 5 and 6, and Colossians 3 and 4, for example. And here again in Titus 2 and 3: how we behave towards one another, then how we are to face the world.

Here is what he says in Titus 3, in a nutshell. Paul says: the gospel demands that we be devoted to good deeds, not divisive and difficult to deal with. That's the overall thrust of this chapter I think. This is what should inform Titus's pastoral strategy as a bishop or apostolic delegate in Crete. It's also a great message for us, in whatever ministries we may be engaged.

We see at the end of chapter 2 that Paul tells Titus to exhort and rebuke people in Crete with all authority, and let no one disregard him. Then in Titus 3:8 he says, 'The saying is trustworthy, and I want you to insist on these things.' The trustworthy saying about the gospel of salvation makes an insistent, authoritative demand on those who are saved. It trains us, motivates us and pushes us in certain directions. It doesn't save us and then leave us to work out what to do next. It doesn't save us and then urge us to follow the changing tides of worldly morality. The gospel has its own insistent demands on our consciences, related to God's unchanging law and His perfect design for the flourishing of His creation.

What does it demand? It demands that we be devoted to good deeds. So in verse 1, Titus is to remind the people to be submissive, obedient and 'ready for every good work.' And verse 8, again he insists 'that those who have believed in God may be careful to devote themselves to good works.' And at the end, in verse 14, 'Let our people learn to devote themselves to good works.' So it's obvious that the gospel demands that we be devoted to good works—things which are 'excellent and profitable for people' (verse 8)—so that we will help others and 'not be unfruitful' (verse 14).

The gospel also demands that we not be divisive and difficult to deal with. So verse 1 again, 'remind them to be submissive to rulers and authorities, to be obedient.' Verse 2, 'to avoid quarrelling, to be gentle.' Then verse 9, 'avoid foolish controversies... dissensions, and quarrels.' And if anyone behaves in the opposite way, verse 10: 'As for a person who stirs up division...' Again, the main point is clear: Paul says the gospel demands that we be devoted to good works, not divisive and difficult to deal with.

So if we want to be good Christians, devoted to good deeds in line with the demands of the gospel, I think that means two things here. First, gospel Christians should be good citizens. And second, gospel Christians should avoid those who are divisive. Those are the two main applications which fall out of this passage for Titus's congregations and for Titus himself as a pastor. So let's look at those two points, as Paul unpacks them for us.

## Gospel Christians should be good citizens

First, gospel Christians—evangelicals, we might say because the 'evangel' is the gospel—should be good citizens. Now you don't need me to tell you that this isn't always the case. Evangelicals have sometimes gained the reputation of being stroppy, subversive, seditious and insubordinate. For some, being evangelical means one is compelled to be disgruntled and disaffected all the time, and because we're right and everyone else is wrong we are perfectly within our rights to be rude and dismissive about them. But that isn't how Paul says we should be, even towards the pagan authorities whom God has set over us. We're meant to be good news.

As Gerald Bray says in his recent theological commentary on the Pastoral Epistles, there's no sign here that Paul thought the authorities might end up persecuting believers, which probably means it was written before A.D. 64 and the trouble in Rome with Nero and the great fire. So, says Bray, 'Paul seemed to be more concerned that believers might use the excuse that they were citizens of the kingdom of heaven as a means of avoiding their responsibilities on earth, and he was determined to avoid a situation in which rebellion against the state could be seen as the natural corollary of the coming of Christ's kingdom.'[1] Some of the Jews were infamous in the ancient world as revolutionaries against the Roman Empire, always 'rebelling and raging' as Calvin put it.[2] But gospel Christians are not to be always rebelling and raging.

Now don't get me wrong. We will always have something to say to the unbelieving powers and secular authorities. If the government is of the left, we will not be entirely happy. If the government is of the right, we will experience discomfort. If it's in the centre, it won't sit right with us. Because we are Christians, not conservatives or socialists or liberals or democrats or greens. We are something else entirely. The gospel stands at odds with every political system and party in this present evil age (Gal. 1:4), which is blind to the truth and in rebellion against Christ. 'He who sits in the heavens laughs; and the Lord holds them in derision. Then he will speak to them in his wrath, and terrify them in his fury' (Psalm 2:4-5). Paul knows that too. But still he says: 'Remind them to be submissive to rulers and authorities, to be obedient, to be ready for every good work, to speak evil of no one, to avoid quarrelling, to be gentle, and to show perfect courtesy towards all people.'

Imagine if that's how we always spoke about our political leaders. If people said, 'Evangelicals have a reputation for being law-abiding citizens, deeply devoted to philanthropy and charity, always getting involved in local community projects, and lovely people to be around.' Imagine if that's

---

1.    Gerald L. Bray, *The Pastoral Epistles* (London: T&T Clark, 2019), pp. 536–7.

2.    John Calvin, *The Second Epistle of Paul the Apostle to the Corinthians and the Epistles to Timothy, Titus and Philemon* (trans. T. A. Smail; Edinburgh: Oliver and Boyd, 1964), p. 377.

how we were in our online lives. No posts at election time being rude about the candidates, or how they voted in the Brexit referendum, or how orange they are. No rush to judgment and condemnation when the government gets something wrong or somebody in it does something questionable. No joining in with the crass chorus of criticism. Speak evil of no one—even Joe Biden and Donald Trump. Be gentle—even towards Kier Starmer and Humza Yousaf. Show perfect courtesy—even to those we might most strongly disagree with or find offensive.

*Gospel motivation*
Why should gospel Christians be good citizens of this calibre? Well, because of the gospel itself, of course. It's the gospel that demands that we should be devoted to good works, not divisive and difficult to deal with. Because the gospel tells us that, verse 3, 'For we ourselves were once foolish, disobedient, led astray, slaves to various passions and pleasures, passing our days in malice and envy, hated by others and hating one another.' Yes, the world is like that, and our leaders are like that. They are slaves to various passions and pleasures, and social media is naturally going to be full of malice and envy and hatred because the people on it are full of malice and envy and hatred, and it gives them pleasure to express that by laying into others.

Here's the thing we mustn't forget: we were like that too. But the gospel is about being saved from that. Not saved so we can carry on like that but dress it all up in religious fervour or don a dog collar to sanctify our self-righteousness. Verses 4 and 5: 'when the goodness and loving kindness of God our Saviour appeared, he saved us, not because of works done by us in righteousness, but according to his own mercy.' He didn't save us because we're so great, in distinction from those reprehensible people who lead us. We got the leaders we deserved, because we are just like them. But God saved us anyway, despite that. Because He's good and kind and merciful. So maybe we should be like Him, in the way we treat those who are just like we were.

The great seventeenth-century Anglican pastor, William Gurnall (1616–79) once preached at election time: 'No sins lie heavier on God's stomach, and make him more heart-sick, than theirs who stand in high and public place of rule and government.'[3] It isn't that God needs us to point these things out to Him in an email. He knows. He watches. When we see bad behaviour amongst our politicians and other leaders, it should make us tremble in fear, in humility, because, Gurnall went on, 'as magistrates [leaders] are, so we may expect things will go in a nation: There is no one place where we may stand at greater advantage to see what God intends for a people (good or evil) than by observing what rulers and governors his Providence orders out to them.' The whole Old Testament confirms this, 'that when God intended mercy to them, he gave them faithful magistrates; when wrath and judgement, he opened the door for it, by taking them out of the way.'[4]

We are meant to be different as Christians to worldly leaders who have their eyes on the next election rather than on the next life. We don't join in with carnal and profane ways of relating to the authorities—because we have been saved, 'by the washing of regeneration and renewal of the Holy Spirit, whom he poured out on us richly through Jesus Christ our Saviour' (Titus 3:5-6). We have been washed, born again, renewed, changed by God the Holy Spirit. Not because we were so wise and astute as to invite Him in. But because, despite our foolishness and disobedience, Jesus Christ poured out the Spirit on us. We are citizens of a different world, subjects of a different kingdom, not by birth

---

3. William Gurnall, *The Magistrates Portraiture drawn from the Word* (London, 1656), p. 4. cf. 'consider the greatest hopes our enemies have is to ruine us by our own Councels: The time hath been, the plot was to blow up our Parliaments, now they labour to blow us up by our Parliaments; to make our Parliaments, I mean, blow us up by their destructive Councels, and a Nation cannot die of a worse death, then to be ruined by their Saviours,' p. 28.

4. Gurnall, *The Magistrates Pourtraiture*, pp. 19, 22.

or by works, but 'so that being justified by his grace we might become heirs according to the hope of eternal life' (verse 7). We are right with God, with rights to a better life in eternity, entirely by God's grace and mercy.

So this is why we can and must behave graciously and submissively towards the world. Because in and of ourselves, we are no different from them. But 'our great God and Saviour Jesus Christ… gave himself up for us to redeem us from all lawlessness and to purify for himself a people for his own possession, who are zealous for good works' (Titus 2:13-14). When we help others in sickness and distress and any kind of need, we are doing what humans were put here to do—to emulate and imitate the practical kindness of our creator, even when the people we help may not deserve it.

That is our gospel, our good news for this nation and every nation. And that's why gospel Christians should be good citizens, however strong the temptations are for us to behave as the world behaves towards those we disagree with, and those who are not like us. I know Jesus overturned tables. Some of us would enjoy that, if we had the chance. Some of us think it's what social media was made for. But we are to do as Jesus says, not do the things He did when we think it might be fun or cathartic to interpret His actions in our own way and imitate the Jesus who agrees with us. And by His holy apostle, He commands us 'show perfect courtesy towards all people.'

## Gospel Christians should avoid the divisive

So, Christians are not meant to be disobedient and difficult people because the gospel teaches and trains us otherwise. But clearly there were some in Crete, where Titus was ministering, who were just like that. We've heard about them already in this brief pastoral epistle. In Titus 1:10 we heard that 'there are many who are insubordinate, empty talkers and deceivers.' They were 'upsetting whole families by teaching for shameful gain what they ought not to teach'

(1:11). They were devoted to myths and 'the commands of people who turn away from the truth' (1:14) instead of being devoted to good works. They were, rather, 'detestable, disobedient, unfit for any good work' (1:16). That's why here in Titus 3:9, Paul says 'avoid foolish controversies, genealogies, dissensions, and quarrels about the law, for they are unprofitable and worthless.' They don't lead to good works, but to arguments and divisions.

The word for quarrels here, *machē*, is a word that speaks of hand-to-hand personal combat. Although the Christian life is often described as a battle and a fight (in Scripture, and in Anglican liturgy), this word here is not a word that is ever used positively in the Bible of the struggle demanded of a believer. Indeed, Christians are to be the very opposite, *amachos* (peaceable, not brawlers), according to Titus 3:2. Macho machismo is not a Christian virtue, but something we should give a wide berth. Stirring up division has always been something that God hates, along with all Machiavellian 'ends justify the means' approaches: 'There are six things that the LORD hates,' says Proverbs, 'seven that are an abomination to him: haughty eyes, a lying tongue, and hands that shed innocent blood, a heart that devises wicked plans, feet that make haste to run to evil, a false witness who breathes out lies, and one who sows discord among brothers' (Prov. 6:16-19).

The word for the divisive person in Greek here is *hairetikos*, from which we eventually get our word 'heretic.' But 'heretic' has a somewhat different meaning in modern English. In Titus it does not mean someone who preaches a specific heresy or false doctrine necessarily, but 'one who creates or fosters factions,'[5] though they probably do this by means of unorthodox teaching as well as by pointless speculations and separations. It's related to a word for choosing. A heretic is simply someone who chooses to think differently from Jesus and the apostles, someone who

---

5. William D. Mounce, *Concise Greek-English Dictionary of the New Testament* (Accordance edition, 2011), αἱρετικός.

consciously divides themselves off from orthodox biblical doctrine. Thomas Aquinas says in his commentary on this verse that, 'if a person were to maintain that God is not triune and one, or that fornication is not a sin, he would be a heretic.'[6] Anti-Trinitarianism and teaching that sex outside of heterosexual marriage is an acceptable lifestyle for a Christian, are equally heretical in that sense, according to Christian tradition. It is not those who counter false teachings such as those who are divisive, but those who introduce them to the church, hoping to get away with it.

We should also add that divisiveness itself is also a kind of heresy. Those who are always stirring up divisions and rebellions, by means of foolish controversies, personal attacks, majoring on minors, and argumentativeness, are also heretics in the Titus 3 sense, however orthodox their theological statements might be. They could be doctrinally impeccable on paper, and irredeemably fractious in practice. Like the devil. It should get them nowhere with gospel Christians. Because gospel Christians should avoid the divisive.

*Contention and brawling*
There is a whole sermon given over to contention and brawling in the Anglican *Homilies,* one of the foundational formularies of the Church of England. It says that 'Among all kinds of contention, none is more hurtful than contention in matters of religion... In St Paul's time, there was such contention and strife among the Corinthians; and at the moment we have the same among us English.' What does this contention look like? 'For there are too many people, in alehouses or other places, who delight to argue about certain questions, not so as to build people up in the truth but for vain glory, and showing off their cunning. And so

6. Aquinas, *Commentary on the Letters of Saint Paul to the Philippians, Colossians, Thessalonians, Timothy, Titus, and Philemon* (trans. F. R. Larcher; Lander, Wyoming: The Aquinas Institute, 2012), p. 457. Aquinas is careful to note that not all disagreements make the other party a heretic, but only in serious matters of the faith.

un-soberly do they reason and dispute that when neither party will give place to the other they fall to criticism and contention, and sometimes from hot words to further improper behaviour.'[7]

The homily contains excellent advice for those engaged in contending today, adding: 'Let us so read the scripture that by reading it we may be made better livers, rather than more contentious disputers. If anything is necessary to be taught, reasoned, or disputed, let us do it with all meekness, softness, and gentleness.'[8] Yet the homily is not advocating unchallenged tolerance of all kinds of heresies and sins. It is not ignorant of the need to draw lines, and does not neglect to mention that 'brawlers' and 'pickers of quarrels' or 'revilers' are among those numbered with the sexually immoral and idolatrous, as those who will not inherit the kingdom of God (1 Cor. 5:11).[9] As I've put it elsewhere, 'the bad breath of bolshiness is so unattractive and off-putting, as the expression of our inward angsts and un-submissive hearts, that it can only please the devil who seeks to divide us.'[10]

*How to deal with heretics*

How are we to deal with divisive heretics? How should we respond to those who choose to teach an alternative to the apostles—an alternative gospel and an alternative way of living as a Christian? The Apostle Paul says that church leaders such as Titus are called upon to admonish them—to warn and instruct them. They should encourage them to change their minds and repent of their false doctrine, and warn them that if they will not do so, there have to be consequences. That's why according to the *Book of Common Prayer*, ministers in the Church of England are to be 'ready

---

7.  Lee Gatiss (ed.), *The First Book of Homilies: The Church of England's Official Sermons in Modern English* (London: Lost Coin, 2021), pp. 177–8.

8.  Gatiss, *The First Book of Homilies*, pp. 179–80.

9.  Gatiss, *The First Book of Homilies*, p. 181.

10.  Lee Gatiss, *Fight Valiantly*, pp. 197–8.

with all faithful diligence, to banish and drive away all erroneous and strange doctrine contrary to God's Word,' while bishops are 'both privately and openly to call upon and encourage others to do the same.'[11]

First, there has to be an effort to reclaim the false teacher for the truth. He or she must be confronted with their error. They must be gently and calmly given the opportunity to correct any misunderstandings. They must be given the chance to change their mind, or withdraw their statements when they are shown to be contrary to what the Bible teaches. And this must be done with prayer. As Paul says elsewhere, if anyone opposes the gospel the Lord's servant must gently instruct them, 'in the hope that God will grant them repentance leading them to a knowledge of the truth, and that they will come to their senses and escape from the trap of the devil, who has taken them captive to do his will' (2 Tim. 2:25-26 NIV). It's that blunt. False teaching comes straight from the pit. So first, we must avoid false teaching because it is dangerous, unprofitable and useless. Then secondly, we should admonish false teachers and pray for them in the hope that God may grant them repentance.

Finally, what do we do if the false teachers do not repent? Have nothing more to do with them, says Paul. Now at first that sounds as if Paul is advocating even more dissension and splitting up and division. That's actually the last thing on his mind. He doesn't want to cause schism and divisions in the church. He wants to preserve the unity of the church. Because there is only one thing that creates unity in the church, and that is the gospel. The gospel outlined in verses 4-7 of Titus 3. The trustworthy saying is if we are not agreed on the gospel, then we are not united at all. No gospel— no unity.

Some people say that we must have unity at all costs, and that if it comes down to a choice between heresy or schism, we should choose heresy. It doesn't matter what doctrine

---

11. See the *Ordinal* on the ordering of priests, and the consecration of bishops.

you believe, as long as we're all united in the same church, or the same institution. As if the only heresy was thinking that there was such a thing as heresy! Now, as Calvin says, 'we have to exercise moderation in not immediately making a heretic of everyone who does not agree with our opinions, for there are some matters on which Christians may disagree among themselves without being divided into sects.'[12] In the end, however, only the gospel is the power of God for the salvation of everyone who believes. No institution can save us, however united it may be. If there has to be a choice between eternal salvation or ecclesiastical unity, that should be a no-brainer.

*Separation*

Here in Titus 3, the Bible tells us quite clearly that there is a time when separating from others is actually essential. Indeed, there are times when distancing ourselves from others because of what they believe or teach is actually commanded by God. I've written a whole book on the places where the Bible talks about how we should deal with false teaching. It does so far more than you might think.[13] And if there has to be some kind of division as a result of false teaching in the church, when Titus 3:10 comes into play, it is the false teachers who have caused the division. False doctrine is what divides. It's not a personal issue about disliking the false teacher. Personality clashes, or differences of style, should never be allowed to come between us. But false doctrine? Well, false doctrine splits up churches like adultery splits up families. And the person causing the split is the adulterer, the false teacher—not those seeking to be faithful to their vows.

Even if it means the faithful Christian must leave a church or a denomination in the end because of false teaching— it is not institutional unity that matters. Ultimately, the

---

12.   Calvin, *The Second Epistle of Paul the Apostle to the Corinthians and the Epistles to Timothy, Titus and Philemon*, pp. 387–8.

13.   See Gatiss, *Fight Valiantly.*

only unity that counts between Christians is unity in the truth of the gospel. It doesn't matter if I am in the same denomination as another Christian or not; whether we are part of the same earthly institution or not makes little ultimate difference. The only unity that ultimately counts is unity in the truth of the gospel, because only the gospel will save. So it is possible for an Anglican such as me to have more in common with Bible-believing Christians in other denominations than with other Anglicans in the Church of England. Not all Anglicans believe the gospel; many Baptists and Presbyterian people do. What ultimately matters is whether we believe the same gospel, and are 'heirs according to the hope of eternal life' (Titus 3:7), not whether we use the same prayer book or wear the same robes or sing the same hymns. These things may be important, but they are secondary matters.

Indeed, Paul implies that we must regrettably find ourselves at odds with many in our own denomination, and in other denominations: those who teach a false gospel; those who preach a different way of salvation; those who subtly change the good news of Jesus into a licence for immorality, or who reinterpret the Bible to blend in with the latest worldly trend, or who forget that we are called to renounce worldly passions and live self-controlled and godly lives in the present age. Have nothing to do with them, says Paul. Separate yourselves from them, distance yourselves from them because, 'You may be sure that such a person is warped and sinful; they are self-condemned' (Titus 3:11).

That's not a personal attack. It's a theological description. Someone who consciously and deliberately chooses to distance themselves from the teaching of the apostles—we must distance ourselves from them. We can do that with a clear conscience. First, the heretical teacher must be given a chance to recant. But eventually there comes a point when all the admonishing will be to no avail. Then it is incumbent upon us as gospel-believing Christians to have nothing to do with them. By refusing to repent, it is the false teacher himself or herself who has caused the division in the church. By teaching what is unprofitable, it is false teachers who cause disunity, not those who obey this injunction to separate from them.

This is a very painful truth. As we sometimes sing in the hymn 'The Church's One Foundation,' the church is often 'by schisms rent asunder, by heresies distressed.' It is not pleasant. If you enjoy this sort of thing, rather than finding it a nauseating and difficult necessity, then there is perhaps a pathological condition there you may need to explore with the help of a pastor or counsellor. An addiction to controversy and the dopamine hit of ding-dong arguments is a problem, not a heroic virtue. But the distressing of the church by heresies is utterly avoidable—if only false teachers would repent and believe the gospel. That's why Anglicans pray month after month in the words of the *Book of Common Prayer* that 'all they that do confess thy holy name may agree in the truth of thy holy word, and therefore live in unity and godly love.' But no amount of institutional unity or superficial love or outward conformity can patch up the bleeding wounds and spiritual hurts caused by false teaching.

## The Church of England today

So then, like spiritual poison, we must avoid false teaching. With gentleness and careful prayer we must admonish false teachers. And where they persist in their errors, and refuse to repent, with a heavy heart we must avoid the false teachers themselves. Because gospel Christians should avoid the divisive. And church leaders, such as Bishop Titus, should take the lead in this spiritual safeguarding process. Does this have applications for us? Is there false teaching in our midst that we must oppose and perhaps visibly distance ourselves from?

As an Anglican myself, I hope you will forgive me for reflecting on the situation I know most intimately. If you are in another denomination, you may want to consider how these things apply more specifically to you. But I think there is application primarily here for our bishops, who in Anglican polity are the ones called to exercise discipline. (Whose responsibility is it in yours? You really ought to know.) We must pray for them as they seek to do this, because we know many people will react extremely negatively if and when bishops choose to discipline false teachers 'privately and openly' as they are called to do.

*Breakdown of discipline*
One of our biggest problems in the Church of England today (and in many other mainline churches I should add) is the breakdown of doctrinal discipline at the national level. At local level, where parish ministers can act with discretion and authority, discipline can still be applied. But the admonitions to Timothy and Titus about silencing false teachers are sometimes not being followed on a larger stage by those with the responsibility for such discipline in Anglican polity. Article 26 of the *Thirty-nine Articles* says that 'in the visible Church the evil be ever mingled with the good.' Yet that has never been an excuse to let false teaching go unchecked, but a motivation to try and deal with it. The Article continues that, 'it appertaineth to the discipline of the Church, that inquiry be made of evil Ministers, and that they be accused by those that have knowledge of their offences; and finally being found guilty, by just judgement be deposed.' This is good Reformation and Patristic doctrine.

That doesn't mean we need to go actively sniffing out heresy, and meddling in other people's affairs, like an inquisition. It means guarding the flock and responding to public challenges to the doctrine and practice of the church. However, those legally holding the power to do this are not always doing it, or certainly not doing it as effectively as they need to. It is true that one cannot be disciplined in the Church of England for preaching the doctrine of the *Thirty-*

*nine Articles*, which is a good thing; but one could, it seems, get away with preaching almost anything these days.

There could be several reasons for this: the expense of 'heresy trials' and the financial choices this involves; the PR nightmare and fear of adverse publicity; the difficulty of establishing a case; the uselessness of the Ecclesiastical Jurisdiction Measure (1963) and the exclusion of doctrinal matters from the procedures of the Clergy Discipline Measure (2003), which is explicitly for 'Disciplinary proceedings concerning matters not involving doctrine, ritual or ceremony.' Or it could be the fact that some bishops themselves hold erroneous views far short of the standard of doctrine set out in canon law (Canons A2 and A5). Yet some bishops do not even seem to use their 'soft power,' to preach the truth and publicly refute error, never mind engage in effective discipline. Given that heresy is gangrenous, pernicious, and poisonous according to Scripture, why is it so unthinkable that it should be rooted out in the church today? Why are those to whom we have entrusted this task not keener to safeguard our spiritual health and wellbeing?

This failure of episcopal discipline causes many problems. It creates ambiguity and uncertainty about our message and makes people question whether we really believe it. It also means that lower authorities, so to speak, such as congregations or groups of ministers or deanery chapters, will always feel somewhat impertinent and out of their official depth when dealing with unchallenged heresy in the wider church. It is not technically their job to discipline people outside their parish, but the bishops' and archbishops'. Even within the parish there are limits to what can be done without episcopal intervention. For example, Canon B16 'Of notorious offenders not to be admitted to Holy Communion' allows for someone in 'malicious and open contention with his neighbours, or other grave and open sin without repentance' to be refused the sacrament of the Lord's Supper, especially 'in case of grave and immediate scandal to the congregation.' This could allow us to deal with some situations akin to that envisaged in Titus 3. But the minister is not supposed to act on this more than once without referring the whole thing to the bishop, canonically. When bishops fail to act against scandalous individuals or ministers or even fellow bishops who deny the faith or propagate scandalous heresies, not only is it frustrating for those who have to sit by in legal impotence, but it undermines the credibility of episcopal polity itself and brings the faith into disrepute.

The problem is, it is too easy for bishops to entrust the difficult decisions to systems and processes, rather than taking personal charge to prevent false teachers from having positions of responsibility and teaching authority. Yet that is a core duty of our bishops, and we have a duty and a right to complain if it is not being done in line with our publicly acknowledged standards of doctrine and morality. Bishops are often concerned with 'jurisdiction,' with guarding their dioceses from outside interference or administrative infringement; but in reality, some do not patrol their patches *spiritually*, and so they begin to resemble the anarchy of the Wild West, where might makes right and any gunslinger with a blog or a pulpit can terrorize congregations with their calamitous errors.

*Gentle engagement*
What can the rest of us do, in the midst of such chaos? Well, whatever actions we take, we should ensure that they are clearly and evidently linked to the scriptural imperatives that we have seen. That is, if we think it necessary—after appropriate investigation, careful thought, prayer, and godly counsel—to take a particular line of action with regards to false teaching or false teachers, it is vital that we persuasively demonstrate how and why we feel this action is demanded of us by God's Word. We must communicate this in a courteous and sober-minded way with gentleness and humility, remembering that sometimes, not everyone

who disagrees with us is 'an enemy' (2 Thess. 3:15). As Paul said, 'Let your reasonableness be known to everyone' (Phil. 4:5)—which means reacting in a proportional way, not writing off every archdeacon because of the actions of one, or the whole House of Bishops because of the teaching of some. 'Speak evil of no one, avoid quarrelling, be gentle, and show perfect courtesy towards all people' (Titus 3:2). Precipitous, bullish divisiveness for the sake of personal glory or reputation is not only unattractive, but exposes our own warped and sinful motivations for all to see; this is not the way to promote and advance the gospel of Jesus, who gave Himself up for us.[14]

Paul ends his letter to Titus by saying, 'Greet those who love us in the faith.' Those who are living in love and faith can rejoice together in their fellowship, even when they can't meet together physically. That's a truth we have rejoiced in over the last few years, when so much has been on Zoom instead of in person. But one day, we will all meet together in the new creation, to worship and serve the Lord Jesus—if in this world we live in the mercy and grace of His gospel, which demands that we be devoted to good works, not divisive and difficult to deal with.

Please join me, as we close this exploration of 2 Timothy and Titus, in a prayer:

Almighty God,
who gives victory to His faithful people
not by might, nor by power, but by your Holy Spirit:
Grant in your mercy that we may not be ashamed
to confess the faith of Christ crucified,
and to fight valiantly against sin, the world,
and the devil
contending for the gospel as His faithful soldiers
and servants

---

14. This section owes a lot to *Fight Valiantly*, pp. 166–70.

until the end of our lives;
for we ask in the name of Jesus,
who conquered the powers of darkness
and gave Himself up
to rescue us from this present evil age.
Amen.

*Also available from Christian Focus Publications...*

*Daily Readings: John Owen*

Edited by Lee Gatiss

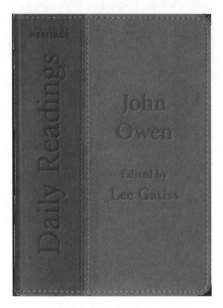

978-1-5271-0720-5

365 daily readings from one of the greatest theologians of the Puritan movement.

John Owen (1616–1683) was one of the best known and most prolific English church leaders of the 17th Century. His writings have been a challenge and encouragement to believers throughout the centuries since and have influenced many leaders in the church today. In this attractively bound faux leather book, Lee Gatiss has selected a reading from John Owen's writings for each day of the year. Theologically sharp, these readings will help you to see the majesty of God anew

Includes some extracts from Owen that are not currently in print anywhere else, and fresh translations of his Latin works.

*Light after Darkness*
*How the Reformers regained, retold and relied on the gospel of grace*
by Lee Gatiss

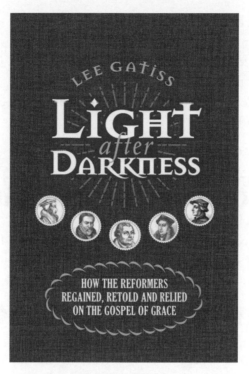

978-1-5271-0720-5

The Protestant Reformers of the sixteenth century regained, retold, and relied on the gospel of grace — and we can learn from their tragedies and triumphs, their dark deeds and noble heroics. The stories of Ulrich Zwingli, William Tyndale, Martin Luther, John Calvin and Thomas Cranmer remind us of the glorious truths which warmed the hearts and fired the souls of passionate and imperfect people, and how they tried to share the good news of Jesus Christ in their generation. Will it strengthen and inspire passionate and imperfect Christians today to emulate their clarity, their courage, and their compassion for the lost?

# Christian Focus Publications

Our mission statement –

STAYING FAITHFUL

In dependence upon God we seek to impact the world through literature faithful to His infallible Word, the Bible. Our aim is to ensure that the Lord Jesus Christ is presented as the only hope to obtain forgiveness of sin, live a useful life and look forward to heaven with Him.

Our books are published in four imprints:

### CHRISTIAN
## FOCUS

Popular works including biographies, commentaries, basic doctrine and Christian living.

### CHRISTIAN
## HERITAGE

Books representing some of the best material from the rich heritage of the church.

## MENTOR

Books written at a level suitable for Bible College and seminary students, pastors, and other serious readers. The imprint includes commentaries, doctrinal studies, examination of current issues and church history.

## CF4•K

Children's books for quality Bible teaching and for all age groups: Sunday school curriculum, puzzle and activity books; personal and family devotional titles, biographies and inspirational stories—because you are never too young to know Jesus!

Christian Focus Publications Ltd,
Geanies House, Fearn, Ross-shire,
IV20 1TW, Scotland, United Kingdom.
www.christianfocus.com